Turning Gray

*A Spiritual Shift,
Leading to Greater Awe of God and Creation*

Well Done Life

Also by Chris Warnky

Heart of a Ninja Series

The Heart of a Ninja

What Just Happened?: The Line

What Just Happened?: The Run

The Heart of a Ninja for Kids

Twelve Traits of a Ninja

Four Traits of a Ninja

Well Done Life Series

How to Refocus Your Life

Search Chris Warnky at Amazon.com

Turning Gray

*A Spiritual Shift,
Leading to Greater Awe of God and Creation*

Chris Warnky

Well Done Life LLC
Columbus, Ohio
2021

CHRIS WARNKY

Well Done Life

Copyright © 2021 by **Chris Warnky**

All rights reserved. No part of this publication may be reproduced, distributed, or transmitted in any form or by any means, including photocopying, recording, or other electronic or mechanical methods, without the prior written permission of the publisher, except in the case of brief quotations embodied in critical reviews and certain other noncommercial uses permitted by copyright law. For permission requests, write to the publisher, addressed "Attention: Permissions Coordinator," at the address below.

Chris Warnky/Well Done Life LLC
1440 Mentor Drive
Westerville, Ohio 43081

Editor: Gwen Hoffnagle
Book Layout © 2017 BookDesignTemplates.com

Ordering Information:
Quantity sales: Special discounts are available on quantity purchases by corporations, associations, and others. For details contact "Special Sales" at the above address.

Turning Gray: A Spiritual Shift, Leading to Greater Awe of God and Creation/ Chris Warnky – 1st ed.
ISBN 978-0-9993331-9-8

Dedication

This book is dedicated to those seeking God with honest, open hearts and minds. It's dedicated to those seeking truth about our existence. It's dedicated to those who have a spiritual relationship with our Creator God yet find themselves asking questions they don't understand the answers to in order to get to know him more deeply. It's written for anyone who hasn't taken the time to think deeply about where we came from, why we exist, and where we're going. Regardless of where you are on your spiritual journey, it is my sincere hope that reading about my journey is thought-provoking, challenging, and encouraging to you as you walk on your own spiritual path.

Contents

Introduction 1

Background 15

    Chapter 1 Context 17

    Chapter 2 My Past 25

    Chapter 3 Early Influencers 33

    Chapter 4 Influencers in Adulthood 43

    Chapter 5 What I've Believed 57

    Chapter 6 A Jolt to My Thinking 65

Seeking Clarity 83

    Chapter 7 Our Thinking 85

    Chapter 8 Seeking More Clarity 95

    Chapter 9 The Bible and Jesus 113

    Chapter 10 Knowing God and Christianity 127

Many More Questions 131

    Chapter 11 Questions – The Bible 133

    Chapter 12 Questions – Genesis 145

    Chapter 13 Questions – God's Design 165

    Chapter 14 Questions – Prayer 185

Chapter 15 **Questions – Church, Hope, and Religions...*199*

Now..207

    Chapter 16 **Wonder *209*

    Chapter 17 **What Resonates Now................................*223*

    Chapter 18 **My Firm Beliefs......................................*229*

    Chapter 19 **A Broader Perspective............................*237*

    Chapter 20 **Pursuing the Big Picture *245*

    Chapter 21 **My Life Now *251*

    Chapter 22 **My Spiritual Routines...............................*261*

Conclusion 269

Learn More 275

Acknowledgments 277

About the Author..279

Introduction

I have been on a highway much of my life, driving 70 miles per hour on cruise control. There isn't much traffic on the road and it's a long trip. I've been paying attention, but haven't needed to concentrate hard to stay on my well-laid-out path, with sharp, fresh, yellow lines on the left and white ones on the right helping me stay on my path and away from any bumpy terrain off to the side. There are often metal guardrails on the right, keeping me safe when I go around sharp turns. There are bright road lights mounted high above to light the way when it's dark.

It's nighttime, and I've been in an accident that has forced me off the highway. I find myself on the frontage road that runs parallel to it. I'm not sure what happened, but I was somehow run off the road and across the grass onto the side road; it doesn't feel like I took a paved exit to get here. But I'm here now.

It was a scary transition, and I don't know where I am or what's going on. I'm a little banged up and my car is damaged, but it's drivable. I'm on the pavement again moving on toward my destination. It feels good to be moving forward again and in the right direction, even though I'm on a service road.

This road goes in the same direction as the highway, but at a much slower pace. Parts are worn and bumpy, there are potholes, and the lines are either faint or nonexistent. I'm still traveling the same general path, but in a much different way, and the journey is not as relaxed, requiring me to stay more alert and intentional in order to stay on the road.

There aren't many others on this side road. I'm taking it alone most of the time, and I miss the camaraderie of the others zipping by me on the highway to my left.

I enjoy seeing the moon and the stars more clearly, since they're not drowned out by the bright highway lights I can see to my left. At this point I'm not sure if I will get back on the highway; I've learned so much from being here, and I sure like the view.

* * *

This analogy comes to mind when I reflect on where I am spiritually as I begin to write this book.

I'm 64, and about 55 years into thinking about the big picture of life as well as my spiritual life. I am 18 months into recovering from a severe concussion I received by flying head first into a wall after hitting a trampoline the wrong way. I suffered tramatic brain injury, or TBI. This is the accident I referred to in my analogy above. Since that time I've been asking a lot of questions about life and my spiritual beliefs. Much that had been black and white for most my life suddenly became gray. (It will take me another 18 months or so to finish writing *Turning Gray*, and my new spiritual journey will have lasted more then three years by then.)

I was convinced that my best next step was to seek truth about the spiritual life, for however long it took to gain greater clarity. The Merriam-Webster dictionary defines *truth* as "the body of real things, events, and facts: actuality." Other definitions include "the actual state of a matter" and "being in accord with a fact or reality." We probably each use this word slightly differently. There is probably no universally accepted definition of truth, but what I'm trying to understand is the way things really are spiritually – what I will call *spiritual truth*.

I have been seeking spiritual truth all of my life. I never want to think that I totally get it and know all the answers regarding life; nor do I believe that's even possible. I think that's far beyond human capability. But I believe we can move closer to the truth. That is what I would like to continually do. I won't arrive, but I sure hope to have moved closer to the truth during my time here. I'm asking many questions I've never asked, but I'm confident that seeking truth is a noble and worthwhile endeavor. I'm able to formulate many of my questions in a clear way, but I'm not clear on many of the answers. I hope you will find my journey interesting and perhaps similar to parts of your own.

Turning Gray

My wife, Carolyn, and I were sitting on our living room couch recently talking about my spiritual journey, and we – maybe she – mentioned that things appeared to be more gray for me these days, especially relative to my spiritual beliefs. She said that she hed seen some of that in her mom when she was in her eighties and nineties.

We joked about the fact that my hair has turned strongly gray over the years. I've had gray hair since high school, and I was definitely aware that my gray hairs had increased during our first few years of marriage, only about five years later. Until recently my Ohio driver's license still said I had brown hair, a vestige from 30 years ago when we moved to Ohio and got new licenses. I have told Carolyn for years that I have brown hair and could prove it because it had been declared by the state of Ohio. But my updated license now states "Gray" hair. Over the years I've absolutely turned more gray.

Since my concussion it appears I've also turned significantly more gray in my thinking, especially spiritually. This analogy of turning gray is a good description of what is going on in my mind and heart – a description that clarifies my thinking and is helpful when sharing it with others. It's a practical word-picture that feels right. Ideas that once fit easily into my life are now less clear, and not as black and white as I have seen them for nearly 50 years. That's a big shift. Until my accident I had not asked myself many questions about my spiritual beliefs, instead just accepting what I had heard as truth. I had not felt like it was okay to ask deeper questions.

Something within me was stirred by my concussion, and I felt pulled along the path to inquiry. As I probed more deeply, my curiosity led to even more questions. Although I still have some strong black-and-white beliefs, my life has transformed from a simple black-ink-on-white-paper cartoon to a live-action gray-scale TV show or movie.

I remember watching the black-and-white TV in our living room as a kid. We watched *Combat*, *The Untouchables*, *I Dream of Jeannie*, *Bewitched*, and many others. I enjoyed being entertained by others' lives played out on the screen. And then one day my perspective changed.

I was so excited and couldn't wait to go over to my best friend Bob Ramsey's house. I had learned that his family had just purchased a color TV. It was going to be an amazing experience to see the shows I had been watching in black and white now in vivid color – at home! I had of course seen movies in color at the movie theater, but not on a TV in a home.

Sitting on the floor watching color TV in Bob's living room was an eye-opening experience. Everything popped out in a whole new way, so bright, so colorful. Everything seemed so much more real and alive. I was glued to it. After that day our black-and-white TV had nowhere near the appeal it had had in the past. I watched quite a few hours of TV at Bob's over the years until we purchased our first color TV.

Turning gray has been as profound as that experience of shifting from black-and-white TV to color TV. Have you turned gray over the years? After reading my story, you might find that you are more gray than you think.

Mindstorming

One day when I was sitting in my favorite recliner trying to bring more clarity to my spiritual thinking and beliefs, I decided to try what Brian Tracy has called *mindstorming*, in which you list 20 ways you can reach your goal or solve a problem. Listing 20 ways forces you to think more creatively than you might otherwise. I usually invest just enough time to come up with two to four options to solve an issue. Identifying 20 solutions takes a lot more time and effort, but it takes me to new and higher levels of thinking.

My spiritual beliefs had been on my mind for well over a year, so I decided to take the time to mindstorm about how to gain more clarity. Sitting there staring toward the ceiling with a blank piece of paper and my favorite pen in hand, within 40 minutes I came up with 20 options for getting clearer on my beliefs. One of them was to write a book about where I am and what I've gone through.

Writing for Clarity

Having already written eight books, I've found that taking the time to write a book helps bring clarity and conciseness to my thinking. When I speak I say what is top of mind. My mind is all over the place, jumping from thought to thought, and that's what comes out when I speak. (Apologies to those of you who know me well and have had to live through these types of conversations.) The good news is that most of you probably communicate the same way most of the time, so you can relate to that way of speaking and probably give me grace in this regard.

When I write a book, I work to provide a good structure to make the reading easy to follow and understand. I also go through multiple rounds of edits to ensure I'm saying what I want to say, and saying it clearly. I've completed at least four rounds of my own editing on most of my books, which always results in thousands of edits. And I usually have at least one person read the resulting draft and provide suggestions. This is a friend who knows something about my topic and is willing to provide me with feedback focused on the content and flow. They often also comment on spelling and grammar. Then comes my professional editor, who provides value in numerous ways, ensuring my content is clear, easy to read, accurate, and enjoyable for the reader, while keeping it in my voice. For prior books she has identified between one and four thousand additional edits to help make my points clearer.

In addition to the benefit to my readers, through this process I personally get clearer on the topic. I like the process of compiling my thoughts, notes, and even what I'm confused about, and then creating a book out of all that, even if it's just for me and I never publish it. I decided this was a good plan in regard to my spiritual beliefs.

The Seed Was Planted

The seed of writing this book was planted much earlier than my mindstorming session, however. Over the years prior to that I shared parts of my journey and my uncertainty with several others in a variety of places: over lunch at Panera; at the reception at a college leadership presentation; during a ninja gym competition; while having lunch at a park; and even with a coaching client before a session. Each time the other person has listened intently, and several told me, "If you gain more clarity, please share it. I would love to read about it! I've had some of those same thoughts and questions and don't know what they mean."

Mark Fitzpatrick, a good friend and a terrific supporter as I've become a writer, suggested I write a book about my spiritual journey. He said, "If it's too personal, then maybe don't publish it. Just writing about it might be a good exercise, and then perhaps you could eventually publish it for others when it feels right." Thanks for the push, Mark. I'm sure your comments came to my mind when I listed writing a book as one of my 20 options.

Carolyn has demonstrated a lot of love throughout my current side-road journey. She would also like the benefit of better understanding what I'm thinking, and an opportunity to talk about it after I have something concrete on paper that's more organized than my mind right now.

The comments from others have been encouraging and helpful as I continue to better understand my spiritual beliefs. It feels good to know that maybe I'm not alone in my questioning.

For years I have read the Bible on my phone using the Olive Tree Bible application, which allows me to highlight and color various words and sections. I highlight in green powerful verses that I feel I understand well and that have been great sources of encouragement and support for me. I highlight in pink sections that I don't understand well or that are confusing. There are a lot of both highlights in my app, and the past three years have resulted in a whole lot more of the pink highlighting, which is further inspiration to resolve some of these doubts.

An Ordinary Man

I'm not a biblical or religious scholar. I'm an ordinary man trying to understand more about this life. I, like millions of others, read, hear, observe, and try to understand how my life fits into this complex world. My interpretation and understanding stems from my personal experiences and training. I completed research on some of the topics I address in *Turning Gray*, but in reality I have been bombarded by so many questions that I have been overwhelmed by the level of research that could be conducted regarding each of them. I don't have the capacity to go much deeper until after I at least get my thoughts oraganized and articulated.

As I move from a strong blind-faith orientation to a deeper, thinking faith, maybe I'm just going through what some call "Christian puberty." In my early sixties I'm going through what some other Christians went through at 16, or when they were even younger. Maybe I'm just catching up with the maturity of many other Christians. My new thoughts might remind you of your own experiences of questioning your faith. Whether it's good or bad to be going through these questions and doubts now, it is happening.

In this book I record my views, not those of all or maybe even many other Christians. They might also have these questions, and maybe they don't think we have all the answers either. Please don't interpret my views as the standard beliefs of all Christians, but I believe it's okay and even benficial to ask good, honest questions, even of God. We are all on journeys of discovery about our beliefs.

My perspective has been very narrow in many ways, and I've had limited exposure to experiences and perspectives that fall outside my Evangelical Christian framework. My beliefs seemed solid and strong, so I really didn't need additional exposure. I saw things the way most of us see things – not neccesarily as they are, but through our filters, views, and expected outcomes. We all think we are being objective, but we aren't anywhere near as objective as we think we are. We can actually be quite blind, including me. This was so evident to me during the 2020 presidential election. Two very different interpretations of what happened and what was said were strongly voiced, declaring very different and often opposite views about the events and statements. We see things the way *we* are – our views fully filtering them – not necessarily as they really are. It's so hard to truly be objective.

I'm sure there are answers to many, if not most of my questions. The challenge is that there are often many answers, and knowing which to trust is the most taxing aspect of my quest.

You might also be searching to know more truth. I hope I continue to search for the rest of my life, because I think there is much more to truth than we could ever fully comprehend. I'm continuing to take baby steps forward in learning more about where we came from, who we are, how we're supposed to live, and then finally where we're going, if anywhere, when we're finished on earth.

Feeling Alone

Throughout this three-year journey, I've had the tendency to feel alone. I keep wondering, *Is anyone else dealing with the questions I'm facing? Especially those with strong Christian backgrounds? Am I alone in my thoughts, questions, and feelings, or have others had some of the same thoughts and sense of awe?* But I do know others who have questions about their spirituality. Most are still pondering and haven't yet spent concentrated time on nailing down answers.

The jury is still out; a verdict has not been reached regarding most of my questions either. I'm trying to figure out how to live while my jury is in an extended period of deliberation in my heart and mind.

In the chapters ahead you will gain a better understanding of what I mean as you read the arguments that go on in my head. I don't know how much I've figured out, but I've spent significant time trying to seek the truth about our existence and the spiritual life.

To My Loving and Supportive Christian Friends

I have many loving, supportive Christian friends. I'm so thankful for each of them and what they've meant in my life. As you accompany me on my journey, it is my sincere hope that you are appropriately and positively challenged to move to an even closer and deeper relationship with our loving Creator, and I don't want you to question your beliefs in a way that would weaken you or your faith.

In certain ways I no longer know how to be around other strong Christians. At times I even want to avoid them because I don't share the same mindset anymore. I fear that some might take my comments as challenging their convictions and beliefs, or as an attack, and that is not my motive.

I hope that *Turning Gray* will help you to know me on a deep level, understand where I am today, and know better how to love, encourage, and support me on my spiritual journey. In turn, I hope to encourage and support you. I love you.

More Motives for Writing

I have a number of motives for writing *Turning Gray* beyond more clarity for me. I have an urge deep inside to document where I am in my journey and share it with those closest to me. I'm being absolutely transparent about my innermost thoughts for this reason.

I also hope to stimulate your thinking on these important topics. I hope to wake you up, if you need to be, to the really big picture of how and why we are here and how we are supposed to live. If you also have deep questions about your beliefs or a desire to have a closer relationship with our Creator God, I would like you to know that you are not alone.

The purpose of *Turning Gray* is not to provide a revelation or to convince you to believe as I do. It's intended to share my personal journey, what I have discovered so far, and where it has taken me. I hope to inspire you and stretch your boundaries. If I were convinced I knew everything about God, I would probably try to be more persuasive. But I'm on a spiritual journey just like you, and hope to convey how awe-inspiring are God and his amazing Creation!

I've tried to share pieces of where I am spiritually with a few people, in just a few minutes, but that has not worked well. It hasn't allowed me to convey the whole picture in the way that writing this book allows. I share over 400 questions I have been trying to better understand the answers to, and most of them I'm asking for the first time. Several have stopped me in my tracks. I can't realistically move forward in my journey while they remain as open as they are for me today.

To read only a part of this book will be to understand only a part of me and where I am on my spiritual journey. If you would like to understand of the whole me today, I invite you to travel with me to the end of the book. I hope your journey through *Turning Gray* will be a continual process of discovery. I have found this proces to be beneficial in my life, and hope you do, too.

Wonder

I use the word *wonder* quite often, and you will see that I use it as a noun – a feeling of surprise and admiration, and also as a verb – to be curious to know something, to ponder, to think about, to meditate on, or to feel doubt in regard to. Throughout *Turning Gray* you will see that I'm continually amazed by God and Creation, so I'm drawn to wonder as I try to comprehend him.

The many questions that surfaced during this spiritual experience led me to much deeper wonder than I have ever experienced about who God is and what and how this universe he created was intented to work. I continue to wonder more than ever about God's design, purpose, and creation.

Love, Mercy, and Grace

I don't spend a lot of time on the topics of love, mercy, and grace, which are so strongly conveyed in Scripture. They are vital for our life on earth as we interact with God and each other, and I don't question the value and importance of these, either spiritually or in relation to our interactions with each other. I focus primarily on the topics about which I'm confused and have questions.

Though the majority of *Turning Gray* focuses on my recent spiritual journey, there are a few chapters about my past that provide background about where I was prior to the concussion that threw me into my questioning mode. I share when things seemed to change, how they changed, and my journey since. I share my increased awe of God, many of my spiritual questions, the ways I've tried to capture and process them, and how they've shaped where I'm now headed.

This book is unique in that I share what I wasn't bold enough to write about prior to my concussion. It's new territory for me, and it's unsettling in contrast to my prior writing experiences.

I quote a good deal of Scripture in *Turning Gray*. Unless otherwise indicated, all quotations are from *The Holy Bible, New Living Translation*, copyright 2015, by Tyndale House Foundation. They are used by permission of Tyndale House Publishers, Inc., Carol Stream, Illinois, 60188. All rights reserved. There are a couple of passages I quote from the King James Version of the Bible, which is the version I read while I was growing up.

Join me now as I share my spiritual journey. I haven't arrived, but I believe I've made some good progress in my continual pursuit of truth.

Background

Chapter 1

Context

Have you ever wondered where we came from and why? Or how we got here? Or about our purpose – what we're supposed to do, if anything? How we are to know if we're being good human beings? Where do our standards and values come from? These are a few of the questions I've asked myself over the past three years. For most of my life I've had simple, standard, Christian-based answers to each of these questions, but for some reason I want to understand them much better and comprehend them with more context than I've taken the time to get in the past.

Many of us live in the moment, in the day-to-day – what has to get done today to survive – and then we move on to the next day. I've always had a great desire to understand my life's context, but my current spiritual journey has taken my curiosity to a radically higher level. I want to know more. I don't expect that I can know the answers to all of my questions, but I eagerly want to know more and be clearer than I am today.

I don't want to just live day to day. I want the big picture. I have loved and tried to honor and serve God, but I want to know him much better – to get a better glimpse of who he is. I don't think any of us can really comprehend much of who God is, so I would be grateful for just a clear glimpse. I sense that he's so much more than I've ever imagined and so much more than anyone I've known has been able to articulate. At times I want to stop everything and just sit and stare at what I can see of his Creation with my eyes, hear with my ears, and feel with my senses; to be in awe of God, what he has done, and what he's currently doing to sustain us each and every day.

Do Our Beliefs Matter?

Below are some key beliefs that have me mesmerized. They stem from teachings in the Bible. In the past I've simply believed these statements and not really thought much about them. Most of my current questions would go away or change radically if one or more of the following beliefs were not true. If you don't believe these you might have different questions and conclusions:

- God is all-knowing, from the beginning to the end.
- God is outside time and space.
- God intentionally designed, created, and sustains everything we know, including our natural laws.
- God is omnipresent.
- God gave us free will – the ability to choose and make decisions.
- Jesus is God and God's Son.
- God resided in the body of Jesus yet was still able to be omnipresent and omnipotent during those 33 years.

Does it matter if I gain greater perspective regarding these? I think it does. I think we live, make choices, and do what we do based on what we understand and believe. Our beliefs tell us whether something really matters or is irrelevant and makes no difference.

We live every second based on what we believe, whether it's true or not. What directs our actions is not neccesarily the truth, but it's what we believe.

I think it's extremely important to gain a solid understanding of what we believe in order to fully know ourselves and find ways in which to grow. If we don't know our beliefs, we can find ourselves simply going through the motions of life instead of living life to the fullest as the best version of ourselves. There are those who feel that nothing much matters, which I think is due to a lack of exploration and understanding of their core beliefs.

Perspective

Our perspective determines what we believe to be possible for us and for others. Our perspective matters, and yet it can be so easy to get sucked into the day-to-day minutiae of life and miss the broader picture. When we live and operate based on the limitations we see, we can get stuck existing in that narrow perspective. If making it to the next hour or day is what we focus on, we'll spend our time on only short-term activities and miss all the potential life holds for us.

Some of us see our lives as if we are the captain of our own little ship out in the middle of the sea with the waves tossing and turning us every possible direction. We are at the whim of the winds and the sea, and we can't see a shoreline or land. We're simply doing our best to stay afloat, not knowing where we're going or if we'll even survive the long trip.

In contrast, some have the awareness to see and experience things from an airplane pilot's point of view – from far above, looking down at the little boat. The pilot has context, or perspective, and can provide instruction to the captain about how to set the sails and the rudder, or which direction to row the boat. The pilot can see the nearest land, how much longer the storm will potentially last, and what direction the boat is drifting. With that perspective and information, the captain can act with intention.

I love that analogy. Seeing things from a pilot's perspective helps me breathe deeply and think clearly. The simple act of staring at the moon provides me with a big-picture context for my life here on earth.

I've heard it said that those who experience life through an hour-by-hour mindset are employed by those who live day by day, who work for those who live week by week, who work for those who live month by month, and so on. The person with the broadest perspective, be it of time or space, lives with the broadest parameters and expectations. They see much more.

I would like the broadest perspective I can get. I'm convinced it will change and improve my life and bring it into much closer alignment with the intentional design of our Creator. As I seek to get closer to knowing him and his perspective, I believe I honor him even more.

The Impact and Power of Awareness

Our perspective is dependent on our awareness – what we see, feel, and know from our experiences. When we're not aware of something, life can happen to us instead of our living intentionally, attuned to our surroundings and interactions.

As young children we're not aware of the danger of cars, so we feel free to run into the street at any time. Our parents work hard to educate us about the danger so that we become aware of it. This awareness is critical to our safety.

Driving

As adults, if we're driving and planning to change lanes, awareness is critical. If a car is passing us on the left and we're distracted or don't take the time to be aware of our surroundings by looking at the side mirror and the rearview mirror and head-checking to our left, as far as we know the lane is clear. We don't see anything because there's nothing in our immediate view, and we therefore assume the lane is clear and the car approaching from behind and to our left doesn't exist. Taking the time to look and see from a few different angles can make a big difference because often what we see immediately in front of us is not the full picture. This translates into seeing the broader picture to make wise choices about how to think and act.

Food

Our awareness about food has a tremendous impact on our feelings, choices, and actions in regard to food. If we're not aware of the nutritional value of our food, we might eat to our hearts' content based only on taste and the eventual feeling of being full. That can lead to overeating and feeding our bodies unhealthy foods, creating various issues for us, sometimes in the short run and always in the long run. If, on the other hand, we are focused on calories and make continual choices based on the number of calories in everything we eat, it can create mental battles, facing the desire for a certain taste while knowing that the caloric content is high – maybe much higher than is good for us.

I am particularly focused on the saturated fat content of foods due to having high cholesterol in the past. This awareness and knowledge has a gigantic impact on my choice of foods and how often I eat them. Our awareness has a tremendous impact on our decisions and the type of lives we live, especially in the long run.

Communication

Awareness also greatly impacts communication. And being aware of how we listen and how we articulate our thoughts has tremendous impacts on our relationships. (Effective communication is close to my heart, and I've planned a future book on this topic with the working title *Enhanced Relationships through Improved Communication*. This name takes advantage of an acronym that matches my middle name, ERIC. I'm hoping to publish it in the next couple of years.)

Health

I was recently reminded of the power of awareness when I had a prostate biopsy due to an elevated PSA test result. I waited the 10 days following the biopsy to hear the results. I handled the waiting period pretty well, but the potential cancer was definitely on my mind. The result came back negative. I was relieved and thankful, but was reminded that awareness is very important.

Some prostate inflamation existed in my body whether I knew it or not. Having the awareness of my elevated PSA caused me to take additional steps to evaluate the situation. My body was the same, but my awareness changed everything. I went through an additional, more complex blood test and then eventually had a biopsy, which, based on the results, could have created even more actions.

Our level of awareness can change our thoughts, our feelings, and our actions. A new awareness can change everything due to the actions we take to influence our future.

Coaching

One of the primary focuses of a coach is to help their client become more aware so they can better deal with their situation and goals. I've seen new awareness change everything over and over again with my coaching clients. I'm convinced that increasing our awareness is vital to living a good life.

As you read *Turning Gray*, I hope you move closer to being aware of your reality and see it a little better than you do today. I don't have full grasp of my own, but I'm discovering more all the time. I don't expect you to land in the same place, but I hope you are able to move further ahead on your own spiritual journey.

Why This Journey Now?

At times I wonder why I'm on this side-road journey and how I got here. What has moved this solid guy, with firm beliefs, to ask so many questions and to become much more in awe of his Creator? Have I been on this journey all my life, moving toward this point that I was going to eventually reach? Did my concussion totally rewire my brain? Did my thoughts and beliefs need to be reexamined or reestablished and this is just the right time for it? Has too much of what I believe not been based on deep thought and reasoning but on blind faith? Have I simply decided that now is the time to think about and understand what I've been saying I believe through years of genuine commitment? Why am I here, and why now? I don't know.

I believe it's most valuable to focus on what we control, not what we don't. Although I wonder why I'm in this questioning mode at this point in my life, I can't dwell on that. Instead I'm focusing on where to go from here. I'm intentional about better understanding my beliefs and why I believe them.

Are you also reevaluating what you believe? If not, maybe my journey will prompt you as a good exercise. It might help you establish more firmly what you already believe and why. This could be a tremendous time of deepening your faith.

Chapter 2

My Past

I believe our pasts tell us a lot about why we're where we are. Mine has had a powerful and positive impact on my life.

I was born and raised in St. Louis, Missouri, in a strong God-and-Bible-honoring family of five. I am the oldest of three kids. I attended church, and became a Christian at age nine when I was baptized.

I lived in Missouri for the first 33 years of my life. My parents have always been strong Christians and believers in a three-part God: the Father; Jesus Christ his Son, the Savior of the world; and the Holy Spirit. They consistently live their beliefs from the Bible – not perfectly, but they've worked hard to honor God through living by the Bible's teachings. The Bible provides great wisdom about how we should live here on earth relative to God and each other. It is the key source for the direction my life has taken.

On a typical Sunday we attended Sunday School at our Baptist church in the morning, followed by a full-congregation church service. We went home for a few hours and then headed back to church in the evening for Training Union, and then another full-congregation church service. I would often remain at the church while my mom participated in choir practice. I also regularly attended a Christian boys' organization, called Royal Ambassadors, on Wednesday nights, which was followed by a church-wide adult prayer meeting that evening. I was a member of the 66 Club, joining those who had memorized and could say, in order, the names of the 66 books of the

Bible. I had it memorized as a thoughtless string of words that I could state so fast you could hardly discern the words. Each summer I was involved in week-long Vacation Bible School programs.

I learned a lot of Scripture from my loving and God-honoring parents and from church teachings and trainings. I learned that the Bible is the absolute Word of God and that nothing can challenge what God declared through it from the beginning of time when he established it.

I was definitely a rule-follower. I did what I was told by authorities in my life: parents, family, teachers, policemen, the law – you name it. My parents told us each December that we were not to go into the workroom in our basement. I just accepted that as a rule, never questioning it or wondering why – it was just the rule. Later I learned that was where they stored and wrapped Christmas presents. I never understood how Santa got the gifts wrapped and into our house. The workroom never came to mind as a place I could sneak into and see what presents had been bought. I also fully believed in the Tooth Fairy without any question.

I never skipped classes in school, high school, or college. I have driven the speed limit all my life; maybe one or two miles over the limit if I'm confident in the accuracy of the speedometer, but not three miles over. I've never had a speeding ticket and plan never to be concerned about that.

My rule-following has come into play in regard to dealing with the COVID-19 pandemic, which is taking place as I write this. Directions from authorities have been to wear masks, social distance, wash hands, and stay at home if you don't need to be out. My family and I have followed these directives more strictly than some of our acquaintances. During times when the directive is to only travel if essential, we work hard to stay at home.

When people in authority have told me to do something, I have usually interpreted it as a requirement, not a suggestion, as some others do. I have accepted what I heard from those in authority and have not often researched why a directive was given. I haven't taken a lot of risks and have seldom pushed the limits.

My childhood was good; not perfect, but good. I was generally a good firstborn, following the rules I had been taught and making a lot of good choices that were consistent with the Scriptures. These choices resulted in countless positive benefits in my life. Things were cut and dry, right and wrong, good and bad, black and white – not gray. I didn't use vulgar, foul, or profane language; dance; drink alcohol; smoke; use drugs; lie; watch TV or movies or read books that contained sex or violence; sexually experiment or have sex before I was married; or buy things on Sunday.

I've always given at least 10 percent of my income (allowances during those early years) to the church or charities. I have never smoked a cigarette or tasted a beer. I received so many benefits from living this way. I believe the structure and discipline of a devout Christian lifestyle prevented me from much potential pain and heartache.

This is what I've known. Biblical teachings have seemed so right, and were infused into my very being. Living by these teachings has seemed consistent with the way our world works. There has been no reason or need to consider other beliefs or ways of living.

Becoming a Christian

At age nine I understood enough of Christian teaching that I wanted to take the next step and ask Jesus to forgive me for my sins. I took the important step that moved me into a personal relationship with God, my Father, who loves me and sent his Son to die for me. Jesus paid for my sins (my wrongs and imperfections) so I could have a relationship with him. In the Christian faith this is referred to as being "saved" or "converted to Christianity." It's a personal process and experience, not requiring any formal blessing or process from a church. This was a major spiritual commitment. It felt good to be forgiven and no longer have my sin counted against me.

Based on the interpretation of Scripture by our Baptist church, soon after I asked God to forgive my sin, I was baptized in the church baptistry, a mini-pool that was installed just at the very front of the church sanctuary. I repeated the words of the pastor, declaring my commitment to God, and then, with both of us wearing white robes, the pastor leaned my entire body into the water and brought me back up again. This occurred in front of the full congregation during a church service. I was formally declaring that I had received forgiveness of my sins and was committing my life to God.

Baptism is interpreted very differently across the Christian religion. We believed it was an act of obedience after becoming a Christian. Some believe you must be baptized to become a Christian. That is why some churches baptize babies soon after they are born. Some believe your full body must be immersed in water and others just sprinkle a few drops of water on you. It's interesting how differently people interpret the Scriptures, and the level of importance they place on those interpretations.

My life didn't change much following that experience. I continued to live a good life, working to honor God, as I had been raised. Unlike some Christians, I didn't come to God after a life away from him. Some have turned to God as adults, seeking and finding him during challenges. I simply followed the natural process of becoming a Christian because I understood what I was being taught and I wanted to go to heaven when I died and not be separated from God for eternity. I wasn't running to him for help for something; I just wanted to be in a relationship with him.

The Baptism of the Holy Spirit

When I was in college I became interested in what some Christians call the Baptism of the Holy Spirit. This belief varies widely among Christians. My parents had this experience and talked much of it while I was in high school. The Scriptures teach that there is an additional spiritual experience, beyond that of receiving forgiveness for sin, that can provide more power for following and honoring God. It's called being filled with or baptized in the Holy Spirit. After months of Bible study and questioning, I decided to ask God to give me this additional power and experience.

It was a significant change for me at that time. I truly gained a greater sense of God leading my life and being present in my life, and greater power to make godly choices on a daily basis.

One of the most evident changes that occurred for me was much better control over how much food I ate. I was now able to eat just enough, and not too much. This demonstrated God's power in a very key aspect of daily life. It was very evident during our next Thanksgiving meal at home. I was simply more content to enjoy the taste of a reasonable portion of food and to then stop and not be drawn into the desire for more and more because of the taste. I had greater control of other areas of my life as well, but my control over the desire for food was the most obvious to me.

Some believe that a sign, or even *the* sign that you have received the Baptism of the Holy Spirit is that you have the ability to speak in tongues, an experience in which you immediately speak a language that is unfamiliar to you. According to Scripture, this is a spiritual language that is given to you by the Holy Spirit. When speaking in tongues, it sounds like another language, but you don't know what you're saying. According to my interpretation of Scripture, it is the Holy Spirit speaking through you and for you, from your heart to God. This capability is a highly controversial topic for Christians. Is it something that can happen today? Is it of God? Is it a good thing? And what value does it provide? Christians have been debating the interpretation of these Scripture verses during my entire life, and surely for much longer.

At the time I asked God to baptize me in the Holy Spirit, I also asked him not to require me to speak in tongues. I had many Christian friends with views on both sides of this topic, and I did not want it to be a divisive element in my relationship with anyone, especially other Christians. About a year later I finally decided I would be okay with receiving the ability to speak in tongues, and that I would keep it to myself so I wouldn't create a controversy among my friends. I received what I believe to be the ability to speak in tongues immediately after that request.

I continue to have this ability, and have used it at various times over the past 40-plus years, usually in times of worship or celebration of an experience God has allowed or provided for me. I have also used it at times when something was deep in my heart and I didn't know how to express myself about it. It is a version of my heart crying out to God for someone or something.

This has been an interesting experience in my life that I really can't explain, like so much of my spiritual life.

The Blessings of Following God

I've observed poor relationships; yelling; and harsh, hurtful comments among people who don't follow God's teachings. I've seen people lie, cheat, and steal, and I've witnessed the bad results from their actions. I've noticed people drunk and not in control of their body or what they say or do. Seeing these things beyond our family convinced me that Christianity is the truth. The Bible is our "owner's manual" from God, informing us about how we're designed to work. I've seen the Christian lifestyle lived out in front of me, over and over, throughout my life. God provides peace, love, joy, and abundant life to those who love and follow him.

What's Changed?

I've lived this way my entire life, and I'm thankful for the benefits I've reaped from living this way. I've not changed the way I live, and I don't know that I will, but I now see things differently. I have begun to question some of the actions and routines that in the past I simply performed on autopilot. I will see where this journey takes me as I move forward.

It's been both exciting and scary to be honest with myself about what I've been thinking and feeling. For months as I sat in my blue recliner, laptop sitting on my legs, leaning back into the chair, I was hesitant about every word I typed about questioning my beliefs. Fear of rejection poured through my body as I tentatively thought, and then slowly dared to type what I was thinking. I wondered, *Are my beliefs true? Am I really thinking these things? Do I really have these questions?* And after a long pause I concluded that I really did. I pushed through the discomfort and uncertainty, slowly typing letter by letter. That feels good in a peculiar way, but a bit like parachuting from a plane – extremely freeing and yet scary at the same time. I haven't yet jumped from a plane, and I don't know that I ever will. But what I feel from this experience must be something like that same adrenaline.

It's weird to be thinking and writing about my past from an outsider's perspective. Like most of us, I've lived inside my own head and world. I haven't seen me from the perspective of an outsider looking in. When I consider the love and Christian training I received, I don't know how I could have believed anything else. I was taught that this was the only truth, and it was black and white.

I'm still pretty much in the same place — not totally, but close. Most of my whites have not turned black and my blacks to white, but there is a lot more gray.

I now see God's Creation as much more expansive than I did in the past, extending beyond us and the earth. When I was growing up, the focus was on us, relative to God. Now I see Creation as much more than the earth, mankind, or me.

I've heard the term *worldview* to represent how one looks at our world. I look at it primarily through my Christian perspective. On this stage of my journey, I'm not sure if I've changed my worldview, but my *view* has become much broader. It seems as though I've transitioned from a worldview to a "universe view," or maybe even better stated, a "whole Creation view." I have a much bigger perspective and it feels so right in my soul.

This new awareness has made it difficult to put any significant focus on the here and now, the earth, mankind, or me. We seem insignificant in relation to the whole, yet at the same time we are a significant part of the whole. This shift in my focus to a universe view makes interactions with those focused on this world more challenging.

Any kid who was raised in my environment and respected authority would surely have become a Christian. There was no other logical option. It would have made sense to anyone. I wonder if I would be Muslim if I had been raised in a Muslim home, or Hindu if in a Hindu home, or an atheist if raised by atheists.

Chapter 3

Early Influencers

As we get older we have the honor and privilege of shaping and molding the younger generation. We should be sure we're making positive differences in their lives and providing them with healthy thoughts that will stay with them for the rest of their lives.

I have been fortunate to know many positive key influencers who shaped who I am. My parents continued to have positive impacts on me throughout my adulthood, but of course not to the extent that they did before I left home at 18. I discuss some other influencers below in a somewhat chronological order.

Sunday School Teachers and Preachers

Quite a few church teachers and preachers influenced my formative years. I can probably name a few, but none of them stand out more than the others. They loved God and loved me and my fellow students. They were giving of themselves week after week to help me grow to know and love God. I'm thankful for them.

Television Personalities

Recently I had an interesting experience that opened my eyes to yet another key influence – television. I was able to list over 140 television series I watched during my first 17 years of life, or at least the

12 years between the ages of 5 and 17. I likely watched well over 2,000 hours of TV as I was growing up. Most of the programming was harmless other than it prevented me from being either more active or more mind-engaging, like reading a book. I sure enjoyed those hours, had a lot of laughs, and still have fun memories about those shows, but it was a tremendous amount of time during which I wasn't developing my mind and growing as a person. I'm thankful for that time, but I also regret that that period could instead have been a tremendous time of learning. Carolyn would likely have been reading books and growing in new ways much of that same time. Think about the impact TV had, and still has, on your life.

New Covenant Fellowship, Ron Tucker, and Kent Henry

Ron Tucker and Kent Henry were worship leaders at the church my parents started attending when I was in high school, and Ron was a youth teacher/preacher/pastor. It was called New Covenant Fellowship (NCF), and it had a gigantic impact on my spiritual life. It's there that my relationship with God became much stronger. I saw many lives changed, and a real focus on worshiping God. I saw people really in love with God – not just going through a weekly ritual. Many arrived more than a half hour early to get a seat near the front and to visit with friends. I've never seen that in another church. I met a number of good friends and I started to read and study the Bible.

Although I attended the full-congregation Sunday morning and Thursday night services at NCF, I also regularly attended the Saturday night youth service with hundreds of other kids in high school or college. Ron was a fantastic teacher who skillfully and interestingly relayed Scripture and its application to life. A lot of what he taught back in the mid-1970s is still with me today. He still preaches and teaches at a large church in St. Louis. Even nearly 50 years later, he continues to positively influence people's lives for God.

Kent was the primary worship leader. He influenced my perspective by focusing on what I consider to be true worship during our singing time, which could last for an hour or more. His teachings connected with my heart and I gained a better understanding of who God is.

Kent led many songs that to me seemed to focus on worshiping God, in addition to some songs about overcoming our life challenges with God's help. He would often lead songs at a much slower pace than usual so we could meditate on the words and worship while singing. I loved the ones that have a slow, repetitive focus on worshiping God, like "Holy, Holy, Holy; I Exalt Thee."

I usually stood about halfway back in the sanctuary, among a thousand others. It was a square, prefabricated building that sat on a large concrete foundation. This was not your traditional church building, but within its walls I found my perfect place – a place of awe, appreciation, and worship. I love being in a place where it's all about God.

I would sway as I sang and meditated on God, with my hands raised high and extended slightly out, and my eyes closed and my feet planted, gently twisting back and forth from left to right with the flow of the music. As the songs coursed through me, I meditated on the words deep in my heart, sensing our amazing God. I still sway to the music every time I get into the message and melody of a song. I think my daughter has picked up on that habit as well.

For over 50 years Kent has had a powerful ministry that has led people to seek and worship God. He has remained faithful to his love and worship of our Creator.

Taking Up Guitar

In my freshman year of college at Southeast Missouri State University in Cape Girardeau, during our early-morning prayer time we prayed for someone to join us who could play guitar each morning when we sang worship songs. I never guessed that I would be the answer to that prayer – a young freshman who had no musical ability or training to speak of. But then I received a guitar, and I learned to play it and to lead others in worship, like Kent had done for me. I used my guitar throughout college and into my first 10 years of marriage to lead people into worship through song.

I've not played much in recent years. I was never good, but I could play six or seven chords, which allowed me to play over 300 worship songs for small groups. I even played guitar and sang to my wife at our wedding. I sang "Let Us Climb the Hill Together" by Paul Clark. And yes, I swayed back and forth with my head up and my eyes closed through much of the song, as I have since late high school, really getting into the words and the tune.

That is me, when I'm engulfed in the words of a song that connect deeply with my heart. The rest of the world fades away as I enter fully into the worship of God. This time is about my relationship with God; or, as at both my wedding rehearsal and wedding, it is also about my deep love for Carolyn.

During the past three years I've returned to a stronger worship mindset, and I sometimes include a guitar to revive that musical experience from my youth. But I see adding music to my spiritual life as one beneficial outcome of turning gray.

Contemporary Christian Music

Contemporary Christian music, as it was referred to at the time, may have had the biggest impact on my spiritual life starting in college, and to this day. I loved the sounds and the words that were true to my heart. These musicians and groups most significantly influenced me: Keith Green, Paul Clark, Phil Keaggy, 2nd Chapter of Acts, Larry Norman, Randy Stonehill, Tom Howard, Petra, and The Way. In more recent years newer artists have impacted my thinking and worship, including Chris Rice, Chris Tomlin, Michael W. Smith, and Matt Redmond.

Most of the songs I listened to were recorded on 33-speed vinyl albums or cassette tapes. You might have heard of these. About 15 years ago I converted most of this music to digital recordings so I could listen to them again. I had stopped listening to them for a number of years because of the effort required or the lack of equipment for those old formats. When I started listening again, I was surprised by the positive, strong, God-loving, and God-honoring lyrics that had filled my mind during my younger years. These songs shaped much of my thinking and spiritual beliefs, and I am forever grateful for them.

Keith Green

I first heard about Keith Green in college. I don't remember how I was introduced to his music, but somewhere along the way I purchased his album *For Him Who Has Ears to Hear*. Keith was electric! He was a forceful and positive influence for Jesus. He was fully dedicated to Jesus. I saw Keith perform in concert twice. He boldly conveyed his beliefs about Scripture.

He also produced a lot of teaching tapes through Last Days Ministries, a ministry he established with his wife, Melody. I would often listen to his music or one of his teaching tapes and say to myself, *I'm not sure he's right or that that's true*. Then I would listen again and think, *You know, maybe he's correct*. Then I would listen a third time and usually come away thinking, *He's right on!*

One of my favorite songs from Keith is titled "To Obey Is Better Than Sacrifice." He produced at least seven albums before he was tragically killed in a small-plane accident in 1982. The loss of Keith was extremely hard on me and on countless others who really looked to him for insight about Scripture. I've memorized the lyrics of many of his songs and they've significantly influenced my life.

Paul Clark

Paul Clark is another significant influence. He's a softer and gentler musician whose lyrics reveal his heart. I have quite a few Paul Clark albums and I still love to listen to his music. One of my favorites is "Serve the One You Love."

Phil Keaggy

Phil Keaggy is "Mister Guitar." He's really fun to listen to and his lyrics hit home. He produced many albums, some instrumental. My favorite songs of his are "Time," "I Love You Lord," and "Your Love Broke Through," which was written by Keith Green and Randy Stonehill.

Christian music of the '70s and '80s had a major impact on my thinking and my life, and I'm thankful I had that exposure. It has been very beneficial.

College Friends

In 1975 I headed off to college at Southeast Missouri State University, known as SEMO. I was about to learn who I really was away from my parents' oversight. To that point I had been a solid young Christian man living by the Bible and the way my parents had taught me. I lived a good life, the way they wanted me to live. Now I was going to be living on my own, over two hours away, in an apartment shared with two freshmen guys I had never met and who were not Christians. I was curious to find out who I really was on the inside when no one was looking – at least not my parents.

Everything was for the first time, and I was doing it on my own. I walked the campus, entered various university buildings, and walked the halls trying to figure out where I'd be going for classes. I searched for places to eat. I had almost no commitments those first few days. I could spend my time in whatever way I liked, and I knew there would be consequences for each choice I made, both good and bad. I didn't go away to college with a friend or buddy; I was there by myself. How would I react to this newness? What choices would I make, totally on my own?

In my first week I fell into a group of people who would significantly impact me for the rest of my life. These were SEMO students who were active at the First Baptist Church of Cape Girardeau. I attended a "Welcome Day" on campus and visited their church booth, which led to my attending that church the next Sunday morning. I fell in love with them through the strong support and love I received from these 50 or so students and the adult leaders who supported this college group.

I joined the choir and began participating in, and helping to lead, a daily 30-minute early-morning prayer time in a room at the church. That's right, every day. Eight or ten of us would attend, depending on our school schedules and other commitments that came up. There were probably 15 of us altogether.

I was also invited to join a five-member musical ensemble. Many of my new friends were music majors. At my suggestion we named ourselves Miracle. Without significant musical background, I felt it was a miracle for me to be singing in front of audiences with only four others.

I grew extremely close to these college friends. They became my new family. I felt safe, loved, and supported every time we were together in my brand new environment. To this day I love to interact with them and see how they're doing. They played a major role in my finding out who I was, on my own, with no one looking. They helped me embrace the spiritual life I would be living on my own. I grew in my spiritual and biblical knowledge – and I hope wisdom – during that time.

We learned, sang, prayed, and played together. I remember shooting a lot of hoops on the basketball court with them and, on our limited incomes, driving down North Kingshighway to Burger King for a Whopper or two. We used a lot of Buy One Get One Free coupons.

I can no longer name all those great friends, but I must acknowledge a few: Larry Young, Debbie Thurmond (Young), Sheila Halford (Youngblood), Glenda (Ellis) and Linda (Heiden) Estes, Cathy Brand (Rutledge), Allan Foster, and Laurie Paulding. There were numerous others, but these friends significantly influenced my life. Thank you!

Carolyn May

I transferred to Southern Illinois University–Edwardsville before my junior year. In my senior year I met a bright, attractive young woman at Christian Student Fellowship meetings. I met several nice women in the group, but Carolyn May was the one I was particularly interested in getting to know. I distinctly remember one night as I sat there in Bible Study: I stared at her, a little to my right and across the table – of course when she wasn't looking. I thought, *I wonder what it would be like to kiss her.*

Less than a week later I was able to answer that question. I think I was supposed to be more focused on Bible Study, but I was a college senior and naturally had interest in the opposite sex. She was the vice president of that student-led Christian organization. There were adults overseeing the group and teaching us, but the officers were students.

I quickly discovered she worked at the library, and suddenly I was visiting the library a lot more often than I had during my first three college years. I "just so happened" to run into her many of those times at the library.

A little later, at a group gathering we both attended, I asked her out to another group activity the next night. (There are some fun stories about our first evening with that group, but I'll leave them for another time.) After that first date we began to see each other daily.

I worked hard to be patient, and held off asking her to marry me until we had crossed the two-month mark. We had to coordinate a time for the wedding when Carolyn's parents would be in the country, as they were missionaries in Ecuador. That date was five months later, the day after our college graduation ceremony. I was a bachelor for less than a day after graduating from college.

Carolyn has had a tremendous impact on who I've become over the past 40-plus years. It would take another full book to write about the ways she has helped me become a better person. She has been a growing Christian since she was three years old. She has a strong grasp of Scripture and she seems to retain a lot more of everything than I do. Our hearts have been aligned spiritually during our entire marriage. She is often my reference when I think about a spiritual point and can't remember where it's mentioned in Scripture. She usually knows the location and can provide context and the point of the message. She has also been a tremendous role model, regularly reading Scripture and discussing it with others, and often attending women's Bible study groups. She has also been a role model in serving others spiritually, and with our financial giving decisions. I'm so thankful for our unity, the strong spiritual support she provides, and the role she plays in my life.

Chapter 4

Influencers in Adulthood

My thinking and choices as an adult have been significantly impacted by organizations, quite a few authors, and friends.

The John Maxwell Team, Paul Martinelli, and Christian Simpson

Over 30 years after marrying Carolyn, when I was close to retiring from the corporate world in 2013, I decided I wanted to become a professional executive and life coach. I wanted to retire, but also be able to provide coaching services part time. I decided to join the John Maxwell Team (JMT) to be trained as a professional coach. This company provides training and certification in leadership concepts, coaching, public speaking, conducting mastermind group sessions, and marketing.

I attended my first JMT live event in February of 2013. Speaker after speaker conveyed their desire to add value to people's lives. Near the end of the three-day event, the president of the organization asked the entire support staff of the hotel – those who had been serving us over the past three days – to come up onto the brightly lit and decorated stage. This included the servers, cooks, conference coordinators, janitors, audio-visual team, and several others. As they made their way to the stage, he led us in a round of applause, and over 500 of us stood, clapped, and cheered for over a minute as the workers looked out over the audience and shed tears in response. The hotel coordinator was given the microphone to comment. In tears, she shared her appreciation for this gesture, stating that neither she nor her staff had ever experienced such gratitude. Tears came to my eyes as well as I participated in that round of applause and appreciation for those who had served us. My heart melted. I wanted to become like these people who appreciated and valued others. This was a dramatic twist from the environment I had been working in, and I will never forget how it made me feel.

When the sessions were nearly over, I texted and then called Carolyn to tell her I wanted to join the mentorship level of the program because I wanted to spend more time with these people and become like them. I was impressed, and felt so loved and supported. They're a hugging group, and they constantly talked about adding value for each other – and took action to do so. I wanted that orientation in my life. Carolyn could sense the impact they were having on me by the tone in my voice, and she blessed the additional investment required for me to move into a deeper relationship with the group.

When I got back to my office in Columbus, a friend stopped me in the hall and asked about my experience at the event. The best way to summarize the difference between the two environments was that at work I felt like I was constantly facing an "I caught you!" mindset. In contrast, at the JMT group it was "I got you." They covered your back and made sure you were supported whether you succeeded or failed. The contrast was so sharp! I wanted to be a part of that supportive environment.

I had already read 14 books about coaching, but I wanted to validate my knowledge and skill by going through a certification process. I was actively engaged in the organization for about three years. I joined the next-level program, the Mentorship Team, and was invited to be a member of the President's Advisory Council. That was a wonderful experience. They were an unbelievably supportive and like-minded tribe. I've never met another group like them, and I miss my engagement with them. At times want to reconnect, but they're heavily focused on leadership training, which I love, but it's not my primary current focus.

The John Maxwell Team is not a Christian organization but it's filled with Christians and like-minded people. I've met many terrific friends there, and many are pastors or former pastors who have retired and moved into leadership training.

The organization's former president, Paul Martinelli, who is a fiery leader and displays a lot of passion, influenced my understanding about how everything is made from tiny building blocks. God holds them together through the way he's designed them. Paul also influenced my belief about our natural laws, created by God, which he refers to as "perfectly and completely established." They're always true and produce the results our actions dictate – always! JMT's former coaching mentor, Christian Simpson, is a quiet and confident guy who helped me step back and look at what I genuinely believe, versus just believing and not being clear about why. I appreciate the value that both of these men brought to my spiritual awareness. The rest of the team and faculty also provided a great deal of value for me during those years. Being a member of the JMT has been a fantastic experience of encouragement, support, and friendship.

Authors

I never read when I was a child! I didn't like books. At times I really hated reading. I was into sports from grade school through high school, and I didn't care about school.

In seventh grade I came home with five Ds on my report card. That wasn't acceptable, so my parents put some major clamps on me and limited my sports activities. (I wouldn't be happy with a child who was getting bad grades because he didn't care either.) My restrictions included no TV – which I really liked, no sports outside with my friends, and no sports on the radio or TV. I loved to listen to Atlanta Hawks professional basketball games on the radio. The Hawks moved from St. Louis to Atlanta when I was in grade school, and I had fallen in love with them when they were in St. Louis. It was a big loss for me not to be able to listen to those basketball games.

To improve my grades, I was also required to read for 30 minutes a day. Reading became my enemy. It stopped me from playing with my friends and playing sports. I now know what my parents were trying to accomplish, but I hated that requirement. It drove me further and further away from reading to *have* to do it. I pretty much hated reading till I was about 45.

About 20 years ago, during a long drive to visit my parents in Wichita, I had a life-changing experience when I listened to an audio book that introduced me to new concepts about how to be a better manager. I was bitten, and bitten bad. I bought the printed book and quickly read it, marking it with my pen and highlighter, making notes in the columns, and turning down page corners. I couldn't get enough. To this day I still don't love reading, but I love the concepts that are conveyed through the written word.

After having read only about four books during my first 25 years of life, I've now read over 500 books, and I want to read so many more. I've become a totally different person through reading. Authors are now some of my closest and best mentors, even though I've never met most of the authors I've read. I relate to them and love their books and ideas. Carolyn and I have debated whether a mentor can be someone you don't know personally; I see these authors as my personal mentors.

Several of my favorite authors have greatly influenced my life. They include Marcus Buckingham, James Allen, Jim Rohn, Matthew Kelley, Maxwell Maltz, John Wooden, Stephen Covey, Jerry Sittser, and John Maxwell.

Moses, Isaiah, Matthew, Mark, Luke, John, Peter, and Paul

The teachings of these biblical figures have greatly impacted me throughout the 17,000-plus days I've been reading the Bible. It's interesting that I can't add Jesus to that list, because he didn't author any document that I'm aware of. Many of my beliefs have come from the few minutes when I've read Scripture in the morning during most of my life.

As a junior at Southern Illinois University, I decided to try not reading my Bible for a month. It was going to be a weird change, but I was curious to see what would happen. After the 30 days I discovered I didn't feel as sharp when it came to making choices and decisions. After that experiment I decided to go back to my habit of being in the Bible daily, and I have done so for most of the past 42 years.

Marcus Buckingham

Marcus inspired me to start reading books so I could learn helpful concepts. His book *First, Break All the Rules* is where my reading started during that trip to Wichita. His concept of helping people be the best they can be, based on how they were created, had a major impact on how I managed others thereafter. That book, and his others, focused me on developing my strengths and those of others versus working on things I don't naturally do well.

James Allen

James Allen wrote *As a Man Thinketh* in 1902. It's a power-packed, 70-page mini-book that explains how our lives are impacted by what we think. He used the analogy of planting seeds in a garden, which is simple to understand: If you plant corn, you get corn, not something else. He made many bold, thought-provoking points in this little book, and it quickly became one of my favorites. I've read it numerous times and have recommended it to many others. I've even held book club discussions referencing it.

Jim Rohn

I think I discovered Jim Rohn because he was often mentioned in *Success* magazine. He had a major impact on *Success's* former Chief Editor, Darren Hardy. When Darren shared insights in the magazine, he would often cite that they came from Jim Rohn.

I've read some of Jim's books, which are very good, but my primary exposure to him was through his teaching CDs, in which he shares many excellent concepts like "Work harder on yourself than you do on your job." He focuses on developing yourself, which provides benefits that last a lifetime. His teachings are easy to listen to and provide down-to-earth practical advice on many topics. I've listened to several of them over and over.

Jim cites Scripture, but without using religious terminology. He would say, "The old prophet once said...," "It has been said...," "A teacher once taught...," and so on. These are almost always followed by an idea that comes straight from Scripture. If you know the Bible, you immediately see the connection. If you don't, the concepts probably sound like creative examples to learn from.

Matthew Kelly

I learned of Matthew Kelly through references by Marcus Buckingham, whom I mentioned above. Mathew shares concepts that are easy to relate to. His book *The Rhythm of Life* is especially good, and *The Dream Manager* is fantastic. One concept that has really stuck with me is that although it's good to always plant seeds for something you want in the future, some seeds don't take root well unless it's the right season.

He also encourages us to dream of things we would like to do someday. He challenges us to document our dreams and share them with others while we strive to achieve them. I have defined and shared 100 of my dreams. I've realized well over 40 of those dreams, and they have been energizing and life-expanding.

My opportunity to hear John Maxwell and Jim Tressel speak in person was the result of taking the time to think through those 100 dreams of what I would like to experience or have and sharing them with Carolyn, my boss, and others. One day when I returned home from work, Carolyn asked me, "How would you like to check off two of your dreams this week?" I smiled and replied quickly, "I would love it!" I asked, "What are you talking about?" She said, "I heard on the radio that there's going to be a leadership summit in Columbus on Friday at which both John Maxwell and Jim Tressel will be speaking."

My eyes lit up! I already valued John Maxwell's teachings. And I had fallen in love with Ohio State football, especially the leadership and tone displayed by the coach, Jim Tressel. Was this really happening? I had taken the time to list my dreams and share them, and now I was experiencing the benefit of someone else being on the lookout for ways they could be achieved. Fantastic!

I asked my boss if I could take a half day of vacation that Friday so I could attend the summit. He responded with a quick "That would be fine. It sounds excellent, and you don't need to take vacation time. We'll fund it as a developmental opportunity." Wow! I was quickly learning the value of Matthew's challenge.

We have a natural desire to help others experience their dreams – *if* we know what they are! This was a clear example of how that natural process works. Taking the time to identify my dreams and share them has brought me many benefits.

Maxwell Maltz

I first learned about Maxwell Maltz indirectly through the leadership summit mentioned above. During a break in the sessions I was determined to try to meet Jim Tressel. I gathered my notes from John's speech and made my way out of the narrow row in the balcony. I crossed over to the stairs, headed down to the main floor, worked my way through the crowd and over to the short set of steps, and walked up onto the stage. Jim was talking to a couple of others when I approached. My heart was pumping. I was already excited about hearing these two speak in person; both experiences were on my dream list. Check, check. Now I was potentially going to have a conversation with Jim. I loved the way he approached coaching the Ohio State football team, and I really admired the way he approached life.

I wanted to ask him something thoughtful and respectful rather than a typical football-fan question. I knew he was a devout Christian, so after a short introduction and a kind statement about his leadership I asked him, "Besides the Bible, what book or books would you say have had the greatest impact on your life?" He paused for a moment and looked toward the ceiling as he responded, "Good question." After a second or two he said, "I think I would have to say Zig Ziglar's book, *See You at the Top*. It's a fantastic book that has been powerful for me." I thanked him and wished him well in the upcoming football season, and then I was on my way, off the stage, freeing him to speak with the next person who was waiting behind me.

What a great experience! I was able to hear Jim speak, meet him in person, and even get a helpful tip that led to further insights. I bought a copy of the book and devoured it. It was a fantastic read with many helpful points, perspectives, and examples. (I highly recommend it!)

In *See You at the Top*, Ziglar cites Maxwell Maltz and his book *Psycho-Cybernetics*. Maltz was a plastic surgeon who studied how our minds work. Because the title sounded so "psycho-ish," I didn't read it for several years, even though several friends recommended it. When I finally read it I discovered a lot of excellent insights into how we think, and it had a surprisingly big impact on my beliefs. One of his major points was that we never act inconsistently with how we see ourselves. That book is packed with powerful concepts, analogies, and stories.

John Wooden

John Wooden, the UCLA Basketball Head Coach from 1948 to 1975, was a proven leader. This is reflected in his 10 NCAA National Championships, unmatched by any other coach in the history of basketball. He developed what he called his Pyramid of Success, which conveys powerfully effective life concepts. He shared with others his personal experiences regarding how to live life, honor God, and develop people and teams. John's ideas have been a tremendous inspiration to me and others. I relate strongly to his definition of success: "Success is peace of mind that is the direct result of self-satisfaction in knowing you did your best to become the best that you are capable of becoming." And I've often shared with others his quote that reflects my beliefs: "There is a choice you have to make in everything you do. So keep in mind that in the end the choice you make, makes you." This is true everywhere I look.

Stephen Covey

The late Stephen Covey captured my interest with his book *Principle-Centered Leadership*. After reading this book I evaluated and then modified many of my behaviors as I increased my confidence in making principle-based decisions, even when they differed from what leaders around and above me advised. This was a thought-provoking book, and I've enjoyed several of his other books.

Jerry Sittser

A couple of Jerry's books had a significant impact on my beliefs relative to learning and following God's will. In *Discovering God's Will* he made the point that if we know Scripture, we know God's will; the big challenge is to live it. This contrasts with trying to *find out* what God's will is in regard to which job to take, person to marry, city to live in, house to buy, career to pursue, etc., as his will is stated right in the Bible.

Jerry shares that if we're anxious about something, we're already out of alignment with God's will, because the Bible says, "Be anxious for nothing." Jerry encourages us to seek God, trust him with our lives, and be the best person, spouse, parent, worker, and supporter we can be – all of which we're instructed to do in Scripture.

I've read, or tried to read, some other religious authors, but Jerry has influenced my thinking more than any of the others.

John Maxwell

I read my first John Maxwell book, *Thinking for a Change*, in 2000, and became even more convinced that how we think is critical to how we live our lives.

I had always liked the quote by Henry Ford: "Thinking is the hardest kind of work – which is probably the reason so few engage in it." I was convinced that spending good quality time thinking was potentially the best way to invest my time; so as a compensation department manager, I began scheduling thinking times, somewhere away from my office but in the building or somewhere on the property. I would sit for an hour or so with a pen and a blank pad of paper, and stare ahead and think about what our department was doing and how we were doing it, where the biggest challenges were, and how they might be overcome. My staff learned that when I came back from these sessions, changes would likely be coming. I would want to try some new process or eliminate a step in an existing one to see if it would improve our performance.

I got my hands on anything that might help me learn how to think better. I really liked *Thinking for a Change*, so I read another of John's books, and then another, and another. I made numerous notes because I identified with his concepts and the points he made. I've now read over 30 of his books. My two favorites are *Today Matters* and *The 15 Invaluable Laws of Growth*.

As I mentioned earlier, I joined the fantastic John Maxwell Team. I heard him speak several times and had some personal conversations with him. He has had a significant impact on my thinking and my beliefs.

Friends

I'm so thankful for each of my friends who have had a positive influence on me. I want to highlight two who have been both friends and accountability partners. They are Bob Valtman and Shanon Paglieri.

Bob Valtman

Bob has been a friend for nearly 20 years. He was a pastor at a church we attended, and is now retired. Bob and I started meeting as accountability partners years ago. For nearly 10 years we met weekly and shared how life was going. We each designated specific areas of our lives in which we felt it would be helpful to have some accountability, and helped each other improve in those areas.

Near the end of my corporate career, sitting across the table at a Panera where we were having breakfast, I was venting about feeling unsatisfied in my corporate role. Bob leaned over, looked me straight in the eyes, and said, "You should be a life coach." I told him, "I've never heard of a life coach. What is it?" He said, "Look it up." When I did so later that day, my heart came alive. I felt like I could breathe more deeply. I was so excited about learning how coaching worked and how I could support others in this way that I bought, read, and marked up 14 books about coaching. This was me – my heart – and I wanted to learn all I could. Ever since that time my coaching knowledge and experiences have impacted my life and the lives of my clients and friends for the better.

Thanks, Bob, for your support, encouragement, and pushes at critical times.

Shanon Paglieri

I've known Shanon for just a few years. We met while training as ninjas at Movement Lab Ohio. We started out comparable in most ninja skills, and we were often in the same group during classes and would train together during open gyms. We became great supporters and encouragers of each other.

Shanon played a major role of support and encouragement when I first started writing books, by confirming, "You can do this!" And she has provided countless tips for my books. She was my first beta reader for my first several books. She is a caring, supportive friend, so I felt safe with her providing feedback. She gave me over a thousand helpful suggestions to improve my first book, *The Heart of a Ninja*. I had been leaning toward naming it *The Mind of a Ninja*, and Shanon encouraged me to change it to *The Heart of a Ninja*. That name turned out to be the perfect beginning for my ninja book series.

Shanon was also a beta reader for this book, and I felt perfectly safe having her read about my spiritual journey and advise me about the writing.

She loves thought-provoking quotes and concepts, and we have a lot of fun sharing them with each other. In late 2017 we talked about how much water we were each drinking each day. We were both quite short of the recommended guideline. We decided to become accountability partners in regard to drinking more water and clear liquids, so now we're "drinking buddies"! We are a couple of years into our accountability and I've consumed so much more water than I ever would have without her. Based on what I've read, getting these additional ounces of fluid each day is good for my health.

Thanks, Shanon, for your friendship, joy, smiles, support, encouragement, and accountability over these past few years. I really appreciate it, and I appreciate you.

These key influencers have all significantly contributed to the person I am today. Thanks so much to each of you who have helped mold my blessed life.

Influencers can be good or bad for us. I focused on the positive influencers in my life, and I encourage you to do the same.

Chapter 5

What I've Believed

Although some of my influencers aren't professing Christians, I've remained a strong Bible-believing Christian, doing my best to follow God and honor him based on the teachings of the Scriptures.

My Core Beliefs

Through the first 61 years of my journey, these have been some of my core spiritual beliefs:
1. God is all-knowing.
2. God is outside of time and space.
3. God created the heavens and the earth and sustains them.
4. God is omnipresent.
5. God is all-powerful.
6. God is holy (set apart).
7. We are to worship God.
8. We are to love God with all our heart, soul, mind, and strength.
9. We are to enjoy the life he has given us.
10. We are to be excellent stewards of what he has given.
11. We are to love our neighbor as ourselves.
12. We are to reveal, reflect, and tell others about our Creator/God.
13. By nature, people are sinful (selfish and self-serving).

14. Non-Christians are separated from God because God has not forgiven them for their sins.
15. Jesus came to earth and sacrificed his earthly life to pay the price of our sin so we can have a relationship with God the Father. God sees us as holy because of what Jesus sacrificed.
16. To honor God, we are to listen to and obey the Holy Spirit.

Questions, Wonder, Doubt

Faith is believing things that we can't see. When it comes to spiritual beliefs, we must have faith because there is so much of the spiritual life that we simply cannot see. Doubt, wondering if what we believe is really true, asking questions that we don't understand the answers to very well... I believe we all have some level of doubt about our spiritual beliefs. It's natural, okay, and how we were designed to work. It doesn't matter if you are a Christian, a Jew, a Muslim, a Hindu, or a combination of various religions and beliefs. We all have some doubt. And some, maybe many, have a tremendous amount of doubt but still associate with some belief system or religion despite their doubt. Perhaps they were raised in a certain way and it's much harder to depart from that practice than to stay associated with it, as it's supported strongly by their family members, friends, or community. It doesn't seem to hurt them, and it's practical to do so, so they stay with the association.

I have had a strong belief in God for most of the past 55 years and I've also had questions, wonder, and doubts. Prior to my current experience of wonder, I lived with maybe a 2- to 5-percent level of doubt about at least some of my core beliefs. Not a lot, but some. My recent experience has led to more doubt. My faith isn't gone, but I have a lot more questions about some of my core beliefs.

A Deeper Look

For the first time I'm trying to understand more deeply what I believe and why. As I think through my spiritual beliefs, I realize there are many facets I will never understand well.

Faith has been a natural, inherent part of my life, but now I want to understand more about it. I feel the need to take this journey farther down the side-road to see where it leads. It's scary, like a trail you might take that leads to a place you don't yet know, especially if you are convinced it's a long trail.

It reminds me of the Tunnel Mountain Trail that Carolyn and I took in the fall of 2019 in the city of Banff in Alberta, Canada. We wanted to see the hoodoos at the end of the trail, which are interesting rock formations that have a thin shape reaching to a peak 20 or 30 feet high. We knew generally what we might see, but we didn't know exactly what these hoodoos would look like in person. It was a cloudy afternoon and there was the potential for rain later in the day. The hike was a 3.6-mile loop with more than a 750-foot elevation gain.

We're in our sixties, and we don't live at altitude. Banff is at about 4,500 feet elevation, and we had hiked a lot that week already, so we were quite sore to start with. After some discussion we decided we were going to take on the trail and discover our way to the hoodoos.

The hike was enjoyable as we made our way up and down a series of dirt-based slopes, though the terrain was more up than down. We saw some breathtaking views of the mountains, and a river to our right. It continued on and on, and it began to feel like it would never end. We wondered if we had it in us to make it to the end and then all the way back. Our bodies ached with soreness.

When we looked up we could see dark, heavy clouds heading our way. Should we keep going and try our best to get to the end, or turn back? We decided to push through, step by step, working through our aching legs and hoping we wouldn't get stranded on the path during pouring rain.

There were some beautiful views, but there were also flat meadows that eventually blended into the background and felt boring. We faced another climb and decline, walking along a narrow ridge. Our pace slowed as we inched closer and closer to our destination. Did I have it in me to lift my leg one more time over a root sticking above the dirt on the worn path? Could we make it? We hoped we remembered correctly that there was a shuttle at the top that could take us back to the start of the trail. How we hoped that would be true.

Finally we arrived at a viewing area where we could see the hoodoos, and they were impressive. Although there were only a few of them, unlike the massive number we had seen in Utah at Bryce Canyon National Park, it was worth the long, wearing trip.

We were beat! There was another short trail a little beyond that point that included a sharp incline but provided an even better view of the hoodoos from a little closer. Did my legs have it in them to make that additional climb for a possible better view, a possible better photo opportunity? I didn't know if I could make it – or make the return trip if there wasn't a shuttle.

I decided that if I had come this far, I should do whatever it took to see the last view and take a photo or two. I pushed onward while Carolyn stayed back and rested, reading the signs that described the history of the hoodoos.

Finally I made it to the last view. It was nice, and it provided a better angle and view than the lower spot. I was glad I had pushed through, and now it was time to either find a shuttle bus or start the hike back.

Carolyn told me how much she was dragging and that she wasn't sure she could make it all the way back down. I explored the campground at the top, trying to see if I could find where there might be a shuttle bus stop, but I couldn't find one. We decided the best plan was for me to hike back, get the car, and drive back to get her. I wasn't sure I could make it down, potentially another two-hour trip to the car. It started to drizzle as I started down the path. This was going to make it even more interesting; I didn't have rain gear. I feared I might get drenched as Carolyn searched at the top for a place to stay out of the rain.

In my mind I began creating stories about how bad it would be if I weren't able to get back to our car. I began to experience what it would be like to be stuck, drenched with rain, somewhere in the middle of the trail when night fell. I wouldn't be able to proceed, so we would be stuck overnight with the wild animals. Snakes came to my mind, adding even more fear. I wondered if we would survive the night or if we would be attacked by predators. Knowing we were in another country made it even more frightening.

Part-way down the path, I turned and saw Carolyn coming toward me. She had decided she was going to go ahead and join me and find a way to push through, as long as we took it slow and rested along the way as often as we needed to. We hoped we wouldn't get drenched.

Slowly, with quite a few rests, we made our way all the way back to the trailhead. The rain had thankfully stopped during the return trip. By the time we got to the bottom I was so beat I could hardly move my legs. I'm sure Carolyn felt the same. But we had made it to the end of the trail and seen the hoodoos, *and* made it back to our starting point. Boy, it sure was a taxing experience.

I was glad we pushed through, but it was hard to constantly stay on the trail, slowly going forward and not turning back before we had arrived at our destination. We saw some fantastic views during that long and taxing trip. The journey, with the highs and lows, was worth it.

I believe my spiritual journey is as valuable, if not even more valuable – just like the hoodoo trail – than the destination, which today is unclear. I'm confident I'm approaching this path with the right attitude: seeking more truth. I'm convinced my path will take me closer, even if I need to take a few side-paths along the way.

Why I've Believed What I Believe

In the past I believed what I was taught, and it seemed consistent with my observations of the world. I had never seriously considered any other perspective or way of believing. I didn't need to, as my core beliefs made sense and were working in my life. I'm just no longer sure that's enough.

Just because I believe something doesn't make it universally true – only right for me, at that moment, in my eyes or my mind. I think this is the same for all of us. What we believe may or may not be true, but through faith we believe it is.

Rather than simply having faith, I want to explore the substance of my beliefs. Believing this or that just because someone told me it was true is no longer good enough for me. I greatly appreciate the value I've received from my past beliefs, and most of what I believed in the past still seems true to me. But now I want to better understand those beliefs and make them rock-solid. I'm willing to acknowledge that my beliefs may have changed.

I believe that living by the teachings of the Bible is the best and correct way to live based on how we're designed to function. I've received so much peace and so many blessings from living in a Bible-based, God-honoring way. I've avoided many issues that torment so many others, causing them to make poor, non-Biblical choices, and destroying their lives. I've been unbelievably blessed by the absolute peace and love I receive; the good relationships I have with family and friends; our peaceful, loving home; the strong work ethic that was instilled in me; and countless financial and material blessings. From a human perspective, how can I possibly argue against the blessings I've received? I can't. The bottom line is that I attribute all these blessings to my loving God and to the teachings of the Bible.

What I've Not Understood

I've also had questions about the Bible and some of the religious instruction I've received, including the biblical teachings of Jesus, Paul, and others. I've not understood or been able to fully believe some of them with my whole heart. These were side concerns, not worth pursuing or evaluating, so I let them go while I moved along, generally living my Bible-directed life.

There have been times I've prayed for direction and haven't seemed to receive it, including how to handle a challenge at work, and looking for the right church for us. Other times I've prayed for others, even over a long period of time, and have not seen the results I requested. An example of this is when my mom dealt with debilitating sciatic pain for months, which was not alleviated by my prayers. I've prayed for me and my family in times of pain or need, and not seen change or results from what I've asked: Carolyn in pain battling "false brain tumor," or tumor-like pressure in the brain; me fighting through months of lingering colds; me with my years of TBI recovery; and my daughter, Michelle's, challenges with throat problems. I was perplexed by not seeing results from these prayers, but not enough to cause me to question my faith.

Now I'm taking the time to understand, and some of my questions have become roadblocks I must work through to move farther down the path of knowledge and relationship with our Creator.

Pursuing questions about your spiritual beliefs is a weighty exercise, but it can provide profound insight. It can change your thoughts, attitudes, and actions, creating a new and different future for you.

Chapter 6

A Jolt to My Thinking

In 2018 I experienced a whole new way of trying to think and understand. It's surprising how emotional I get when writing or reading about this experience; it takes me right back to the emotions I felt at the time. This chapter is an overview of my traumatic experience, to give you better context about how and why my journey changed. The impact to me has been much greater than I would ever have imagined.

I started training to be a ninja in 2014. I'm referring to the sport of *ninja warrior*, or indoor obstacle-course racing, based on the popular NBC TV show *American Ninja Warrior*. During my first four years of training I developed a good deal of ninja strength and skill.

On the evening of March 7th, 2018, during a ninja class, I hit a trampoline wrong, which shot my body forward in an unexpected way, and my head smashed into a two-by-four wall support. Three layers of my forehead skin were ripped open, from the center of my right eyebrow to the top of my head – about a four-inch curved rip, clean down to the bone. It looked like I had been scalped, but my skull wasn't cracked.

I remained awake and alert through the whole ordeal, not fully comprehending the magnitude of what had happened. Those who were there said I talked rapidly, probably in some form of shock. All that I knew was that I had hit my head hard and that it stung. When I put my hand up to touch my forehead, I was surprised by the amount of blood dripping into my hands and then down my face and forearm, and I felt confused. The significant flow of blood seemed excessive for a little bump on my forehead. Wasn't it just a bump? Both the staff and several ninja friends went quickly to work, supporting me as this unexpected experience played out before us.

I was taken immediately to the hospital for surgery. It was my first time in an ambulance, the first time I was admitted to an emergency room, and the first time I had emergency surgery. In the ambulance I answered the paramedics' questions. I thought I was doing fine other than the bump. The paramedics decided to lift my head and neck a little and put a neck brace on me.

I told them about the Ninja Lite class I would be teaching at noon the next day, which was a clear indication of my lack of understanding of the magnitude of my injury. To my surprise they said, "You won't be teaching any ninja class for several days." I didn't get it. What was the big deal? In my mind, other than the blood, this was just like any other bump I had previously incurred at the ninja gym. One paramedic added, "You have multiple surgeries coming, starting tonight." *Really? Me? For a bump?* was all I could think.

I closed my eyes and rested as I waited to arrive at the hospital, continuing to try to process what was going on. I felt no significant pain and couldn't figure out why everyone was overreacting.

At the hospital I was wheeled out of the ambulance on a gurney and rolled into the emergency room. I felt the thump, thump as we rolled over the threshold of the hospital entrance. I was experiencing what I had seen on TV, watching the ceiling panels pass over my head. They cut and removed my black "Ninjaworks" T-shirt from my chest, asking me question after question. There were about five medical staff huddled around me as we moved down the hall. I also learned for the first time what it's like to be rolled into an operating room. I had made it to age 61 without any of these experiences, which all changed that night.

The surgery went well. They stitched three layers of skin back together. The next morning I completed a concussion evaluation with an occupational therapist, and passed – not perfectly, but I was deemed ready to go home. They gave us a concussion assessment to complete at home a week later, and I was discharged before 24 hours had passed.

I had an extremely laid-back recovery week, not doing much other than sleeping and eating. A week later, when I completed the home concussion assessment, we found that my condition was worse. I was facing concussive side effects. My thinking was unclear, my eyes were sensitive to light, and sounds were often too much.

Struggling to Recover

My body continued to heal, but I still couldn't think very clearly or make many decisions. When Carolyn asked, "What would you like for lunch?" or "What restaurant shall we go to for dinner?" I couldn't deal with multiple options. I couldn't think clearly enough to make a choice. It was unbelievably hard and caused significant pressure in my head. I could answer yes-or-no questions, but choosing among options was actually painful!

The head pressure was constant. It felt like I had an extremely tight bicycle helmet strapped onto my head, with the strap tightened three or four inches too tight – but only on the left side, which felt stranger still. I'd never had headaches, so I didn't know what they were like and wasn't initially aware that that's what I was experiencing. I simply felt a lot of head pressure that impeded my concentration. I thought to myself, *Maybe this is a headache.*

I had a hard time with loud sounds, and something that normally sounded soft or even just slightly loud now sounded way too overwhelming. I had to get away, get ear plugs or something. I couldn't stand it. To control my exposure to noise, I seldom left the house. When we watched TV I wanted the volume turned quite low.

I tried to go to church once or twice, and the volume, especially of the music, was way too much for me. I felt the pressure mounting in my head, getting tighter and tighter when the bass guitar and the drums were played. I would cringe as I anticipated the next beat of the song, knowing more was coming. Eventually the pressure drove me out of the auditorium, and sometimes even out of the building.

I also found that I couldn't process multiple people talking simultaneously. I couldn't distinguish the person who was talking to me from other people who were talking in the room. This happened at home, at restaurants, and at hotels and church meeting rooms. I couldn't tolerate being in the church lobby because of this issue.

I had further challenges at home when we had the TV on while someone was talking, or if multiple visitors were talking at the same time. I remember having friends over to watch a football game and some *American Ninja Warrior* episodes. It was a good idea to lift my spirits and see my friends, but it didn't work. I just couldn't handle group activities and often found myself in sensory overload. Everything was jumbled together, and when I tried to concentrate on what was being said, the pressure in my head increased. I would have to retreat to a calm, secluded place to recover.

Most light was too much as well. As much as I love sunlight, I couldn't handle it during those long months of recovery. I wore sunglasses to watch TV because the screen was too bright, and sometimes just around the house. I was sensitive to all forms of light, and a light that I once wouldn't have even noticed now caused significant head pressure.

When I tried to read, I found I couldn't hold on to the information or process it in my mind. Grasping any point took so much concentration that when a second concept was introduced, the original concept dropped from my mind. I couldn't read a long sentence or multiple sentences and understand what was being conveyed. One day I tried to read a short spiritual devotional, but I couldn't understand how the first two sentences were linked. I read the first sentence and thought I understood it; then I read the second sentence and couldn't remember the concept from the first, so the sentences remained unrelated to one another in my mind. I got confused and frustrated each time I tried. I soon gave up in disappointment and discouragement. Reading wasn't an option for that stage of my recovery. This lasted for several weeks.

It was hard to not feel good, not be outside of our home, not be in a different environment, not interact with others, and not read. For months all I could do was sleep, lie in bed, or lounge in a recliner, sitting up just long enough to eat. I wore sunglasses everywhere I went.

Television

TV had not been a major part of our lives up to that point. We watched one or two one-hour shows a week, maybe a movie, and some sports, especially on the weekends. The TV wouldn't be on for more than four or five hours a week. Now watching TV was all I could do. There were quite a few days when I stayed reclined for 18 hours or so. For a break I would watch four to six hours of TV.

I had heard TV was mind-numbing, and now I can testify to that. When my mind wouldn't work, or work well, the only thing I could handle when I was out of bed was watching a TV show, movie, or sporting event. We don't have a TV in our bedroom, so going to our family room to watch TV provided a needed change of environment. Needless to say, my TV watching increased radically.

During the nearly nine months I was at that level of recovery, I searched for new or different TV shows to watch just to survive the boredom. My friend Bob Valtman suggested I try *NCIS*, which I hadn't seen, and Carolyn and I watched many episodes together.

I also came across *NCIS: New Orleans*. Carolyn didn't care for that one as much, so I watched it without her. We had normally watched TV together, since it was more like a treat than something we did all the time, and we wanted to share the experience. So I had to get used to watching by myself. Over those months I watched four seasons of *NCIS: New Orleans*. I often watched them between 2:00 and 5:00 a.m. because I couldn't sleep or stay in bed any longer. I knew sleep was important for my healing, but I needed a break.

NCIS: New Orleans helped me make it through those most difficult months. I never would have dreamed that that would happen. The cast became my friends. I came to appreciate the dedication of Dwayne, the toughness of Gregorio, the Alabama background of Christopher, and the strong and yet soft side of Loretta. It didn't matter if I was distracted or didn't understand everything that was going on; it just gave me something to do that wasn't sleeping.

I also watched several Amazon Prime free movies on TV. They weren't my favorites, but they were something to watch and try to follow. I found myself emotionally engaged with the characters, bringing me to tears several times, which really felt good. This was probably a good outlet, as I was feeling discouraged and frustrated about my situation and the slow pace of my recovery.

One night I watched both *The Notebook* and another tearjerker. I sat there in my recliner with my legs curled under my heated blanket and was drawn into each character, the emotion they were portraying, the dilemmas they were dealing with, and the sadness they experienced when a loved one declined or died. I cried and cried. It felt so good! I needed the release from my disappointments and frustrations. This occurred several times over the months when the tension I was feeling inside would build due to my lack of recovery progress.

TV was the only media that worked at all for me. It didn't matter if I missed some or even a lot of the plot; the pictures and actions provided clues about what was happening – if I stayed awake. The goal was to pass time and heal, not learn or comprehend anything complex.

Gatherings

Group gatherings, especially loud, joyous, or fun gatherings, are still hard on me. Like most people, I enjoy getting together in large groups for parties, family gatherings, watching games, and going to games or events. But these group activities are now too much for me to take in and process. I almost always use a coping strategy during these "fun times" that are no longer fun for me.

This is evident while visiting with my parents and family. I've always enjoyed making trips to Wichita to visit my parents on a key birthday or for anniversary celebrations. There is often extended family there, and the gatherings can get loud. Post-concussion, these interactions have become extremely difficult for me. Soon after others arrive, I step into the hall or a distant room down the hall so I can still hear at least a little of what's going on and feel connected, even if it's from a distance. Due to the sensory overload, I can't be in the middle of the party. I fear that others will think I'm not being social, but they understand that it isn't personal.

Listening from a distance is one of my coping strategies for auditory overload. I have also found other ways to limit the effect of overwhelming sound. Using one of my four styles of earplugs, and moving to the back corner of the room, are helpful. Most often I need to leave and go to a place that is quiet.

Reading

As I mentioned, for several months I couldn't concentrate well enough to read and absorb much of any content. After working for a couple of months with an occupational therapist on the coordination of my two eyes, there was some improvement. Once my right eye was able to move and focus on the same place as my left eye, I was finally able to return to reading, comprehending a sentence or two at a time.

We learned my right eye wasn't tracking with my left. The eye doctor told me this had likely been the case all my life, but with the concussion the disparity between the two had worsened. My brain was working hard to get my two eyes to converge on the same thing, especially to track movement such as one word to the next word. Due to the difficulty of the task, I often ran out of energy and ability to comprehend and process what I was reading. This is similar, in a way, to having a bad cold – so much energy is spent on breathing that your energy reserves are too drained to do anything else. Rest and recovery are important for optimal healing to take place.

My therapist had me perform various exercises, and they were draining too. I could only handle so much at one time, as little as 10 minutes of effort. Eventually, with a lot of work and discipline, my eyes started to work better as a team. I was able to concentrate much better on words, sentences, and eventually paragraphs. Progress!

Carolyn tried some of my eye exercises and found she couldn't do them well either. Evidently she has learned to read and operate primarily with her dominant eye. I needed my two eyes to focus together easily and naturally so my mind could concentrate on understanding rather than on the physical act of reading.

This concentration issue extended far beyond reading during the first few months of my recovery. I also tried to listen to content, like church sermons and podcasts, but I had a terrible time following and understanding the points being spoken. Sitting in the back of the auditorium, I heard the pastor's first sentence, and while I was trying to understand it he had moved on to his second sentence, and after that I couldn't catch up. My processing speed lagged, so I couldn't follow the points he was making. My mind couldn't hear, retain, and process how everything fit together. It would have been helpful, but not at all realistic, for him to speak at one-eighth of his usual pace; and that still might have been too fast. I tried to listen, both in person at church and via the recorded video or audio on the church website, but sadly I just wasn't ready to handle even simple concepts, live or recorded.

Deciding

During the first nine months after my concussion, Carolyn and I made a few trips out of town. Sometimes we would be driving during a mealtime and Carolyn would ask, "Would you like to get a quick bite at McDonalds, Wendy's, Arby's, or Taco Bell?" I couldn't concentrate on all those options; it was too much for my healing brain to handle. Carolyn got used to my saying, "You know what I like. Please pick something for me. I can't decide right now. It's too hard. I know you are trying to help by giving me options, but I can't handle it. Please just pick something."

When we went to more formal restaurants, I just stared at the menu. I slowly read the detail of the first menu item, learning that it contained rice and chicken. Then on to the next menu item, which included beef and corn. When I tried to compare the two menu items, I couldn't remember what the first item contained. I would read the first item again, but could no longer remember what was in the second item. Back and forth, I tried and couldn't do it, though I knew how simple it should be. And as you can imagine, most restaurants have 15 to 30 meal options to choose from. It was overwhelming, to say the least. I would again say, "You know the kind of things I like, Dear. Please just order something for me. I can't do this." It was a hard several months before I was able to handle making choices like that again.

Looking back I realize that this injury was more severe than I had thought. It was disappointing and frustrating to acknowledge where I was and how far I had to go to return to my pre-concussion state.

Professional Support

A few weeks after my accident, when we could tell things were not going well and I needed more help than we originally thought, my general practitioner referred me to a concussion specialist. Just getting in to see a concussion nurse practitioner took an additional 30 days. She scheduled me for several therapy and eye appointments. She was also the first person to identify that my two eyes were not working well together.

Physical Therapy

My first physical therapy appointment was quite interesting. It was about eight weeks after the concussion. I wasn't sure what to expect. I was still extremely cautious and sensitive to my body movements, and especially my head. I had finally crossed the threshold of being willing to let the shower water touch the sensitive, injured portion of my forehead, which had felt like I was wearing a plaster of Paris cap. I was very protective of my head, and any touch or sensation there triggered a wave of fear and created tension in my body. I would cringe, fearing the pressure in my head would quickly increase, as it often did.

It was a weird twist. I had a three-by-four-inch section of numbness on the right side of my forehead due to the nerve damage, yet I felt pressure at the edges of my imaginary cap. It was a scary combination of hypersensitivity and pressure on my head. I was afraid of any movement or touch, and began experiencing a lot of negative self-talk at that time. I found myself frequently fearing the worst.

The physical therapist started me with some general movements – a baseline of activity. I handled them surprisingly well. He then put his hands on my head and started to move my head and neck left and right and up and down. It was a shock to my system when he applied this light pressure to my head. While it was scary, I was encouraged that I could even allow him to do it, and I didn't experience additional pain or a worsening of symptoms. I had progressed enough that I could tolerate my head being touched, and it felt good for my stiff neck to finally get some movement.

This was probably the best value I received from my weeks of physical therapy. I had new insight into what I could handle, and it was more than I had expected. I was willing to go through these actions when there was someone there who was trained in what was beneficial and what was too much, but I wasn't willing to go there alone, fearing I could do further harm. I had eight physical therapy appointments over the course of two-and-a-half months.

Speech Therapy

I had four speech therapy appointments over a one-month period, the first about three and a half months after the injury. I had a hard time concentrating when my therapist had me listen to and recite various lists, such as "Red, church, umbrella, elephant, bus," then try to recall them later in the session. I didn't do well. I couldn't hold them in my mind for recollection. I recalled them better by my last session. And she gave me other tests regarding memory, such as drawing shapes from memory.

My speech therapist also helped me address my terrible sleep pattern, which was really hindering my ability to function. I had a hard time sleeping through the night, getting only about two or three hours of consecutive sleep at a time. For the bulk of the night I would lie awake with my mind racing about something I had seen or felt earlier in the day.

It was most comfortable to lie on my left side, with the numb side of my head facing up. I had to remind myself to close my eyes, which oddly wasn't natural. Sometimes I turned to my right side and put my right hand under my right cheek so the most sensitive part of my head was slightly propped up and not touching the pillow. Then I would pull up my knee and stretch out my calf in front of me, then pull it back in and straighten both legs, pull up the covers and then pull them partially down. Getting comfortable wasn't easy. And finally, after lying awake for hours and hours, I would roll out of bed around 9:00 in the morning. I couldn't get comfortable no matter what I tried, and although I wasn't sleepy I was worn out and exhausted from lying down. This continued for quite some time, being awake during the night hours, day after day.

Sometimes I got up in the dark and headed downstairs to our family room. As I mentioned, I watched a lot of *NCIS: New Orleans* in the middle of the night. Once I had seen all those episodes, I moved on to *NCIS: Los Angeles* and started the whole process over, watching past episodes.

The continued sleepless nights wore on me and did not provide me with optimal recovery. My speech therapist shared a list of strategies I could employ, such as keeping a sleep diary, exercising early in the day, and setting a bedtime routine. I was already doing some of them, but I hadn't tried getting out of bed if I didn't fall asleep within 15 minutes. I modified this practice and began getting up when I hadn't fallen asleep within 30 to 40 minutes. This was better than lying awake for three or more hours. She also recommended that I consistently get up early in the morning regardless of how little sleep I had gotten; and I wasn't to take any naps during the day. So I began waking at 8:00 a.m., which made for some hard days of exhaustion. I did my best to come up with anything to keep me awake during the day, including watching a lot of TV, listening to music, nibbling on food, you name it! Eventually this strategy helped me establish a more consistent sleep pattern, and I was thankful for the progress.

I was surprised to discover that the speech therapist addressed these areas for my recovery but speech was never addressed. I wasn't sure how a speech therapist was going to help me because I thought my speech was just fine; I must have been correct. Speech therapy includes much more than I had expected. The therapy was effective, and we both agreed it had accomplished its goals within the four sessions.

Eye Doctor

Based on the concern that my eyes weren't tracking together, I was referred to an eye doctor at Ohio State University. She evaluated my progress while I worked with my occupational therapist to get my eyes to work together. I visited that office four times over the span of five months.

Occupational Therapy

Occupational therapy was the biggest focus of my rehabilitation. I met with my therapist 15 times over the span of five months. We didn't begin working together until nearly three months after the concussion.

The primary issue we dealt with was my eyesight, working to get my right eye in sync with my left. I worked through various exercises, some requiring me to look at double images, each a different color. I was challenged to hold the two images together as one while I slowly moved them farther and farther apart, left and right. That was hard, and extremely taxing. During those months I was able to get my eyes working together much better, which made a world of difference.

I got plenty of attention and support during these several months from those who work in the medical community. I made 47 doctor visits during the year following the concussion.

The Book of John

Once I could read again, I went back to reading Scripture daily, as I had done for the past 50 years. I decided to start with the book of John, which is the book Christians often encourage a new Christian to read first. It focuses on Jesus and God's love.

I started to read slowly, since I was still not processing thoughts well or quickly. I was surprised by how hard it was to follow the first few verses and chapters.:

In the beginning the Word already existed. The Word was with God, and the word was God. He existed in the beginning with God. God created everything through him, and nothing was created except through him.

My mind was trying to figure this out. What was the Word? It didn't say *Jesus* as I had always assumed; it said *Word*. A few verses later it states:

So the Word became human and made his home among us.

I was having trouble processing the references to the Word and all of the *hes*. I tried to piece it together, but it just wasn't clicking. If Jesus was God, I wanted the Bible to come out and literally say Jesus is God, but it didn't. You had to piece several verses together to get the point, if a point was to be found.

I also couldn't understand how God could fit into a man; how the potter could become the clay – even that analogy seemed weak to me. It was more like the potter became one little speck of the clay of a tiny, delicate, detailed pot.

Another analogy that is used is that the Incarnation is like the painter becoming the painting. That no longer seemed to capture the magnitude for me. To say that God came to earth as a man, Jesus, felt more like the painter becoming one partial brush stroke of a marvelous 20- by 40-foot masterpiece. In other words, the partial brush stroke was only a small, undetectable part of the magnificent whole. These were also difficult concepts to process.

I became aware that moving beyond the first few chapters wasn't going to be easy. Rather than reminding me of what I had been taught in the past, it was like I was reading it for the first time, word by word – not even sentence by sentence – though I had read many of these verses dozens of times.

For the first time, the Bible didn't seem right or believable. For most of my life I had verbalized about and connected to Scripture with ease, and now it was as though the black-and-white printed page had turned a murky gray, and the gray was spilling into my spirituality.

The Bible had served me well over the years, so I stayed with it, slowly continuing to read, word by word and sentence by sentence, until I reached the end of the book of John several weeks later. I still had questions, and there were many things I didn't understand or couldn't believe wholeheartedly. This was the simplest and easiest book of the Bible for someone who was getting to know God. I knew

God and had a solid relationship with him, so how could this be so hard?

A New Journey

As I gained the ability to think and process a little more each day, spending time in the Bible continued to be challenging. I still wasn't getting it, and my questions multiplied, so I spent more time trying to figure out what I really believed. For the first time in over 50 years it wasn't sharp and clear. I thought my basic beliefs were still intact, but were they? I was confused regarding something that had been rock-solid for me. It seemed that my rock had become an air mattress, firm but slowly losing air. I wanted to figure out what was going on and how these once-reliable pieces of my life fit with my current muddle. It was exhausting each time I tried to concentrate on the details in question.

The more questions I asked, the more questions popped up — ones that I had never thought to ask. The questions were daunting to my solid Christian perspective, and were taking me into unknown territory. It was hard to accept that I was really questioning my religious beliefs.

I felt both uncertain and determined in my questioning. I resolved to focus on what I could control and let go of what I couldn't. I now had these questions and I was ready to face them. It would have been easier to avoid them, but I wanted to dive deeper to discover and grow in my spiritual life and my relationship with God.

My spiritual life was such a major part of my life and my daily and weekly routines that I knew I needed to deal with these questions that filled my mind. What once was clear to me had become hazy and clouded. I no longer knew how to confidently deal with the Bible, prayer, worship, church, and time spent with other Christians. By shining a light on my state of mind and diving deeper, I hoped to gain clarity about my beliefs.

As you can see from my concussion experience and what followed, survival was, and sometimes still is, my number-one goal. The medical staffs and strategies really helped me survive, yet my thinking changed, or shifted, like it was somehow rewired. This is when my new journey of spiritual wonder began.

Seeking Clarity

Chapter 7

Our Thinking

The more questions I tried to think through, the more challenging questions entered my mind. I was fully enveloped in a sea of gray.

I questioned my faith more broadly and deeply than I had ever questioned it before. I longed for better context for the topics I was questioning. Short, simple, narrow answers that were 100 percent faith-based were no longer working for me.

Some have asked me if I was questioning my spiritual beliefs because God "allowed me to have the concussion." My response was, "Absolutely not!" My concussion was simply cause and effect: I hit a trampoline wrong; it sent me in the direction it would send anything or any person; I hit my forehead on a two-by-four supporting a wooden wall directly in front of me. God didn't do that to me. And he didn't fail to protect me either. He perpetuated his amazing power of having his natural laws of gravity and motion consistently in effect, as they've been since the beginning of Creation. I hit a wall consistent with the natural laws of the earth. God remained consistent and my action created a natural result.

I began to try to figure out my spiritual beliefs from different angles. My first step was to better understand the way I think.

Our Minds

The way God designed our minds is awe-inspiring. Scripture states that God can transform you into a new person by changing the way you think (Romans 12:2):

Don't copy the behavior and customs of this world, but let God transform you into a new person by changing the way you think. Then you will learn to know God's will for you, which is good and pleasing and perfect.

Our minds control our lives. Our thoughts and beliefs lead to our feelings and actions, which create our futures. Understanding and controlling our minds is fundamental to the way we live. This moves me to strongly guard my mind and to intentionally control what I let into it and what I let it dwell on. But I wonder if I take this as seriously as I should relative to its impact on my life.

Henry Ford said, "If you think you can or if you think you can't, you're right." This might not be absolute, but it's true in many aspects of our lives. When we think we "can't" something, we live out that "can't" experience. When we live the "can" experience, though we might be limited by our skills and capabilities, our experiences can be far more fruitful than what we have accomplished in the past. The "can" thinking gives us a tremendous advantage. When we use it, we can also experience "can" beliefs.

I also believe our minds are extremely limited. They simply can't comprehend a lot at one time. It's much easier to focus on only what is immediately in front of us: family, job, possessions, obligations, and whatever it takes to have a good today. Focusing beyond that usually takes too much effort, and we can't see the value in trying to understand more. Our minds are already maxed-out and exhausted by what is right in front of us.

I know my mind is limited, yet I want to comprehend all I can to gain the best possible context for my life. In doing this, I'm confident that I'm thinking, being, and doing what I can to be the best possible steward of my life.

The Thinking Process

I believe our thinking process is designed specifically by God to work the way it does, but I wanted to better understand how it's designed, so I started with the following observations:

- We're actually all people of faith. We believe things we've never seen, such as God/Creator, evolution, and gravity. Our thinking provides us with hope and fear. Both are based on things we have not yet seen.
- We see what we believe to be true or want to see, and our ability to rationalize is powerful. It's involved in how we interpret politics, spirituality, pleasure, dread, right and wrong, cause and effect, and on and on.
- We see things through who we are, not necessarily as they are to others, and we act based on our own perspective – our faith in what will happen next if we act and if we don't.
- The only thing that seems real to us is the thing we're thinking about now, whatever that may be. All else falls by the wayside.
- Our beliefs and thoughts are different from others', which leads to unique actions related to rest, eating, exercise, productivity, relaxation, spirituality, relationships, etc.

I have also come to believe that no one has a lock on truth – we see only our own versions of the world, and that none of us fully comprehends God. We do the best we can with what we believe to be true.

As Romans 12:2 quoted above says, "...let God transform you into a new person by changing the way you think." Our thoughts, and the instruction we get from others, create our view of the world. Our thinking is vital to what we believe, and we do our best to comprehend what's true and what isn't.

We Live in Different Worlds

We're all humans, and yet we each live in our own personal world that we see differently from the way the person next to us sees theirs. I consistently observe this difference in perspective through coaching others. What I see as a helpful solution they might see as a crazy idea that makes no sense and would never work. Why wouldn't my insightful idea or suggestion work for them? Simply, my solution would work well in my world, but not in theirs.

We process life through our own thinking and experiences, so what we do is different from what others do. I would rather watch a YouTube video to learn something, and another person might rather read an owner's manual, and yet another wants to play with it and try to figure it out on their own. Coaching is effective because the coach is trained to use the world the *client* lives in to draw out solutions that will work best for them. A good coach doesn't pour solutions from their own world into their client.

Our worlds are so different because our experiences are so different, which leads to different thinking. We live in different homes; have different families; have worked different good and bad jobs; have had different good and bad bosses; have different kinds of friends, or no friends; have watched a different mix of movies and TV shows; have read different books, magazines, blogs, and posts – or none of these; have received different training opportunities; have traveled to different places; have gone to different religious services; and so on. These combine to create different worldviews. We each live in different places in our minds. To one person, going to an opera is exciting, and to another it's the most dreaded of experiences. (I won't share where I am on this example!) To one person, waiting at an airport or bus terminal for someone is a waste of time and effort, and to another it's a great way to support and please someone, especially someone they love; maybe they like the time away to enjoy reading or to observe others and how they behave.

Even our spouses or life partners don't live in the same world we do. We shouldn't assume that other people's worlds are like ours or that they think the way we do. They probably don't.

The Large House Analogy

God is like a nice large house with multiple floors and a basement. Each of us has a separate version of God based on our own unique perspective. A person standing in the street facing the house might describe it using its exterior characteristics that can be seen from the front, such as the door, awning, windows, and front yard. Because of their vantage point, they remain unaware of anything about the inside rooms or the back of the house.

Maybe another person is under the awning on the front porch, facing the front door. That person doesn't see the second story, the size of the house, the color of the roof, or anything on the inside or behind the house.

Another person might be in the kitchen with a partial view of the dining room. They don't know the color of the outside of the house, what the front yard looks like, or whether or not there's a porch on the front.

Maybe another person is on the roof. They see only layers of dark overlapping shingles and the 360-degree view of the yard around the house. They can't tell you the color of the house or how many floors there are. They might guess based on how high they are above the ground, but they don't know.

Another person might be on the top basement step with the basement door closed. They see only the steps below them, the back of the dark door, and a slight view of the floor of the basement.

Each of these people, based on their vantage point, sees and experiences the same house in much different ways. If you asked each of them to describe the house you would get answers that describe totally different places, yet they're at or in the same house.

This is an analogy of our different understandings of God and Creation. Each of us, including me, sees only a small part of it based on our individual mind and experiences.

I can't tell you which person I would be in this analogy. I feel like my spiritual journey has caused me to take a couple of steps back from wherever I was, so I'm seeing things at least slightly differently than I have in the past, and maybe from a broader perspective. I might be the one at the front door and I've stepped back off the porch to see more of the house, a little of the sky, and a little more of the exterior. I'm still missing so much, but I see a little more.

Our Unique Thinking

We live from what we see in our minds, which is enhanced through our senses. When we hear a noise downstairs in the middle of the night, we might vividly see, in our mind, someone breaking into our house and accidently knocking something over in the dark as they're approaching the stairs to come attack us, and we experience the anxiety of being attacked. Fear kicks in and we might imagine even more detail concerning what could happen. The intruder might have a gun. There might be more than one of them. They're looking for the bedroom to find a stash of money. Our anxiety skyrockets and we tremble and sweat. We try not to move, and make our breathing shallow, concentrating on hearing the next sound. Silence is almost even scarier.

But the sound could have been anything. In some ways it doesn't matter what really happened; what matters is what we saw happen in our mind and the fear we experienced.

Some people live in constant fear due to a mindset that creates situations like this over and over as they move through their days. We can experience what we see in our minds, both to our benefit and to our detriment.

Anything we deeply imagine, we experience emotionally through joy, fear, peace, a sensation, God – you name it. It doesn't have to be true, and it doesn't matter if it's not. If we imagine it we experience that emotion, and might experience it physiologically. For example, you might anticipate having dinner with a good friend, and the tension in your body evaporates, you start to breathe more deeply, and a smile comes to your face. On the other hand, if you're somewhere with your worst enemy, you tense up and you might feel a cold chill in your body. Maybe you're going on a trip to the beach and you can almost feel the warm sun and hear the waves murmuring. The stories in your mind are created in anticipation of how the experience will go. Each thing you imagine results in some feeling – excitement, confidence, fear, etc.

I've experienced this when giving a speech. I prepared well, but my lack of confidence in myself and my ability to convey my message was so intimidating that it offset much of the benefit of my preparation. As a result I left out key points or spoke too quickly, limiting processing time for my listeners, which resulted in a less powerful speech.

When preparing to read out loud in groups, in my head I've created terrible stories about how poorly I will read a passage. I've told myself I wouldn't know a word or words, or would mispronounce a word, or would stutter over words I wasn't familiar with, and that everyone in the room would know. I lived out the experience of my ability being criticized or being laughed at. I've felt the embarrassment of not being good enough for those around me. When I see myself as being unsuccessful, I usually am. When I see myself as having success in those situations, moving forward with confidence, I usually perform well. My actual experience is directly impacted by how I think about it. How I think about something can be even more important to my psyche than the reality.

We see things differently from others because we make different assumptions based on what we have been exposed to and what we choose to focus on. Our natural tendency is to think others assume the same as we do, but just as we all have a distinct and different fingerprint, we're each unique in that we each live in our own world.

The Thinking Cycle

Our thinking process is cyclical:

- Our thoughts and beliefs lead to emotions and feelings,
- which lead to our actions,
- which result in experiences,
- which lead to further emotions and feelings,
- which lead to more thoughts, reinforcing our original thoughts or creating new ones.

If this cycle leads to new thinking, it can instill a greater level of confidence to move us forward; or it can create more fear, hesitancy, or stagnation. We seem to live out this cycle over and over, hour by hour and day by day, as we carve out our futures.

Intentionally changing our thinking or beliefs for the good can have a compounding positive effect on our lives – or the exact opposite can happen as we spiral down into a reserved, stagnant, and negative lifestyle caused by believing the worst. And we all *choose* how to think.

Intentional Thinking

The healthiest way to address our thinking is to stop long enough to evaluate what we're thinking and how it is, or is not, serving us. This is one of the key benefits of being coached, because most of us either lack awareness about how our thoughts affect us, have subconscious barriers to evaluating our thinking, or simply don't take the time to conduct such evaluation. But doing so can change our lives for the better. We can make intentional changes to create and think in ways that facilitate better thought patterns, or "self-talk scripts," as I like to call them.

I've come to believe that most of our actions are actually dictated by our *subconscious* minds. Our thoughts are so ingrained that it often requires no conscious thinking to prompt our behavior; they're a natural part of us. Some of our subconscious thoughts serve us well. We don't have to concentrate to tie our shoes, brush our teeth, get dressed, or type on a computer. These habitual actions make our lives easier than if we had to concentrate to perform each of them.

Automatic behaviors can lead to disaster as well, like taking another potato chip or spoonful of ice cream over and over, yelling at someone because we didn't get our way, and staying on the couch and watching yet another TV show before going to bed. These behaviors continue unless we consciously change our thoughts, and it takes intentional action to transform them. We have to determine what source generated these thoughts, how often and why they surface, and what we're doing to feed them. We have to evaluate whether or not we need to change our "mind diet." This can be done through introspection, interactions with others, or learning how others have done so and trying those methods. Just as our bodies and stomachs react to poor food choices, our minds do the same, and with potentially even greater consequences. As Jim Rohn said, "Quality reading material is like feeding the mind – Bread for the Head."

Our images of God can also become programmed in our minds so that they're automatic rather than considered. We habitually experience that image rather than who he truly is. Jesus is vital to Christians because he revealed who God is in much more detail than the Old Testament did. God is revealed there, but in ways that are more difficult to comprehend.

Chapter 8

Seeking More Clarity

There are several ways in which I've tried to better understand my spiritual beliefs as I continue to drive down this access road alongside the main highway. I've sat for hours and hours in my recliner trying to bring more clarity to the massive number of spiritual thoughts and feelings that have been floating in my head since my concussion. I've often thought something made sense and that it worked with other concepts, and then a contradicting thought bubbled up. While attempting to think through my thoughts, I've often felt overwhelmed.

At times I've wanted to stop, close my eyes, fall asleep, and wake up back where things were on the day before my concussion, but that of course hasn't worked. I keep pushing through and working hard to explore my spiritual world as objectively as I can. We live in both a physical world and a spiritual world, and my spiritual world has played such a vital role in my life that I feel I should thoroughly evaluate it to be sure my thinking is as truthful as it can be. Sometimes I close my eyes to limit distractions while I try to concentrate, and sometimes I stare out the window at the sky while I processed my thoughts.

My Strongest Beliefs

My strongest spiritual belief now is that God is beyond comprehension. He's our Creator and he created much more than our little planet with its inhabitants. We are clueless as to everything he has going on. His design and his way are often difficult to understand.

If, or when, mankind ceases to exist on earth – or maybe when the earth ceases to exist or is destroyed – it will be like one grain of sand disappearing from the universe. It won't be the end of the universe's story – just the end of our story, at least here on earth. We and the earth are like a sentence, a word, or maybe even just one letter in the massive volume of Creation.

God designed and established the powerful natural laws that keep everything going and in place. We repeatedly reap what we sow, or get what we deserve or what we ask for, through our actions. We get what we plant. If we plant corn, we get corn, not green beans or a rose. There aren't many shortcuts in life, if any.

I'm confident about each of these beliefs, but my certainty about many others that I've believed all my life is much grayer.

Working On It

I've shared my questioning with some Christian friends who responded with standard Christian answers that weren't helpful. To accept their answers, I would have to redefine the beliefs I described above. Many pat Christian answers are no longer working for me. I want to know more, to dive deeper into what is beneath the answers my teachers and others provide. Until I better understand the context of these doctrines, I'm no longer willing to accept them. I dread being around Christians who provide responses such as "It's just faith." At one time this would have sufficed, but it no longer resonates with where I am.

I've tried to break down my thoughts in various ways, concluding that our limited minds just can't fully comprehend the magnitude and glory of God – that we can only catch a glimpse of who he is. Here are a few of the ways I've tried to bring more clarity to my thoughts and beliefs, which are described more fully in this chapter:

- I documented over 150 of my current beliefs.
- I listed my most challenging questions.
- I created an "If... then...." document to better understand where I am.
- I created a "beliefs tree" to understand what's behind each of my core beliefs. It dives six levels into my thoughts.
- I created a pyramid diagram showing where I am in my assessment process.
- I developed a "What Jesus said according to John" document to get clearer on the claims of Jesus based on what he is reported to have said and done in the book of John. (See the following chapter for this one.)

Each of these assessments provided clarity in its own way, though they also generated more questions. But structure helps me process everything and brings organization to my floating, unresolved thoughts.

I decided I needed even more structure – a way to capture my seemingly disconnected thoughts and organize them to see what that might tell me. I also hoped that would help me discover which of my various thoughts were similar but just reflecting different perspectives.

I decided it would be easier to move from pen and paper to computerized documents so I could more easily organize my thoughts. I would be able group them, sort them, uncover patterns, and hopefully reduce them to a vital few to provide more clarity.

I entered new territory, creating and exploring questions that I never would have imagined exploring in the past, and finding redundancy in my beliefs, which was encouraging because it seemed to at least reflect consistency. The questions seemed to pour into me and flow through my mind. It was uncomfortable and exciting at the same time.

150+ Beliefs

My first step was to document my beliefs in a spreadsheet, allowing me to review them, organize them, and begin to process them. I didn't want to lose any of them!

I categorized them by *Creator*, *Jesus*, *Prayer*, *Mankind's Free Will*, etc. I also grouped them by my level of confidence or confusion. I grouped them by types: *Statements*, *Questions*, and *New Discoveries*. I even wrote a "So what?" and a "Next steps" entry for each of them. It's a very large and detailed spreadsheet – too large to share here, but I made sure the most important of my 150 beliefs are reflected in *Turning Gray*.

This was a valiant effort to get all my thoughts into one place, but in the end it was still overwhelming, and created more questions. It didn't provide as much clarity as I had hoped. I tried reviewing my list with Carolyn, but the process was slow, and didn't seem to help move me forward. I decided I needed more structure.

The Most Challenging Questions

Among the many questions floating in my head, I was able to document the major ones and sort them by category:

The Earth and Mankind

How can Creation be primarily about the earth, or us? It, and we, are like grains of sand in the grand scheme of things. Focusing our spirituality on the earth and mankind seems self-centered, narrow, egotistical, and wrong! Focusing primarily on our survival – making it through the day – and our lives, feels so wrong! Creation isn't primarily about us, yet very intimately includes us.

God Is All-Knowing

What does it mean that God is all-knowing? Does he know our past, present, and future? Does he know our thoughts, words, and actions before any of them occur?

It's hard to comprehend how a conversational relationship can exist between God and a person. It seems to me that, just as with a person, he wouldn't experience surprise, anticipation, joy, disappointment, and other emotions if he already knows everything before it unfolds; and in his case he knows so much more than a person does. That God is all-knowing is one of my core beliefs, but does *all* mean *all*, or something else?

Our Two-Step System

Why did God establish a two-step existence for people (I'm not sure what to believe for animals): our temporary time on earth, and then a second, permanent existence in either heaven or hell? It seems to me that if he already knows ahead of time the exact experience and result of something he creates at the time he creates it, then he is intentionally designing it that way; otherwise he would have designed it differently for a different experience and result. He didn't have to design a two-step existence for us, so why did he?

God Fit into a Man

How can our Creator fit into a man on our speck of a planet? Did just a part of him enter into Jesus? And if so, how much? What parts? And how did it work? Who is Jesus, really? I don't feel like I'm ready to even approach answering this question. Believing Jesus is who he said he was seems right on most fronts, and yet I have new questions.

Connecting My Beliefs

How can I connect my current understanding about various topics into one cohesive whole – the topics of Creation, the universe, and our Creator; the earth; the separation from God of non-Christians; Jesus; spiritual teachings about sin and forgiveness; and my daily life and actions?

God Changing His Masterful Design

When would God intervene or change his natural and masterful design based on our requests? When would it even be good for him to do so? Based on God's unbelievable design, with countless natural laws – such as the reaping of what we sow, and mankind's ability to make choices – when does he change or override his laws and the choice he has given us? It doesn't seem like he does, at least not very often, or it's beyond my understanding. We're like mites on a grain of sand without true perspective, so how can we ask for anything when we don't know the big picture?

Absolute Truths

What are absolute truths? Do they exist? There are countless natural laws that seem to be absolutes, but if there are prayer-based overrides when God intervenes to change something, then even natural laws are not absolutes.

Each of us defines what we think are absolutes. These vary significantly for each of us depending on our unique outlooks and experiences, so can there even be any true absolutes?

Where do we look for absolutes or standards? How do we decide what they are? What criteria do we use? Even if we look to the Bible, our interpretations of the absolutes in the Bible vary.

Humans Separated from God

Does sin – our selfishness – separate all of us from God? This one is extremely hard for me to answer. In my heart, based on all my past Bible teachings, I would absolutely say yes; we are all cut off or separated from God based on our sin. A Christian is only able to have a relationship with God because they are forgiven of that sin, which was paid for by the sacrificial death of Jesus and by the Christian asking God to forgive their sin that was laid on the person of Jesus.

But while I believe we are sinful and selfish, I'm not clear about how that separates us from God. I believe he sees that we are selfish, but does that cut him off from hearing us, communicating with us, and sustaining us? I don't see that as being the case.

Below are a few secondary questions – important, but not as important as those listed above.

Is This the Design from the Beginning?

Did God design and plan everything this way from the beginning? If he's all-knowing about all of time, including all of life's joys and sorrows, then it would follow that the way things currently are is the way he designed them. Do I believe that's true?

Is God Perfect and Holy?

Other than through the Bible, how do we know God is perfect and holy? Is the Bible the only source for this knowledge? If he weren't perfect and holy, how would the concept of sin and separation even exist? There is much that hangs on whether or not the Bible, which is such a critical cornerstone for how I've believed, is true.

Is the Bible God's Divine Word?

Did God plan for the Bible to come together the way it did, and when it did, considering the conflicts over its content and the battles between various groups wanting to include or exclude certain content over the years?

Is Jesus God?

Is Jesus God, our Creator and sustainer of our existence?

Why Did Jesus Die?

My Christian teachings taught me that Jesus died to pay for the sin of mankind. When I read what is stated in Scripture, it appears he was put to death by the Jews and Romans for calling himself, or being called, the King of the Jews, the Son of God, or God. It was because of who he claimed to be, not because of the Jews, Romans, or anyone else's concern about sin. It doesn't appear that they knew he was dying as a sacrifice for the sins of mankind at the time of the Crucifixion. It seems their motive was completely different. Was his death repurposed or multipurposed?

Is There a Heaven and a Hell?

Is there a heaven and a hell? Do we go to one after death?

The Origin of Spirituality

How, when, and where were fundamental spiritual beliefs first conveyed to mankind? From a documentation standpoint, many were conveyed 3,200 years into mankind's time on the earth, or even later. Examples that come to mind include God as holy, God as Father, Jesus as the Son of God, sin, separation of non-Christians from God, heaven, hell, the prophesy of the Messiah, and forgiveness of sin.

In His Presence

What does it mean when people say "God showed up," "God was with us," or "We were in God's presence"? He's always omnipresent, holding everything together. For him not to be present is for us not to exist.

Evolution

If evolution is true, when and how did people develop thinking, reason, etc.? How and when did it start, and why has it not developed that way for animals as well? I don't understand the progression that is supposed to have occurred.

The answers to these questions continue to confuse me, and I have many more. This is just a taste.

If... Then... Assessment

I conducted an "If...then..." exercise. I fleshed out my beliefs by first stating a belief, then defining the impacts of that belief. What does it lead to? What are the logical conclusions? I did this in order to apply my beliefs more consistently to my life and across each of my other beliefs. It was an attempt to see things more holistically, and as less fragmented.

Like many of my other assessments, this brought more clarity and a lot more questions. It was a healthy but difficult activity. I addressed these core-belief statements:

1. God is all-knowing.

2. God is outside of time and space.
3. God made and sustains Creation.
4. God is omnipresent.
5. God is all-powerful.
6. God is holy.

Below are some results from my assessment.

God Is All-Knowing

If God is all-knowing, *then* he knows the past, present, and future. He knows how Creation began and how it will end – or if it will end. Nothing is a surprise to him. He already knows. This indicates that all of time is by design, since he knew it before it began, and he knows the outcomes of how he created it.

What is prayer, relationship, or communication with him, since for him there would never be new information, discovery, anticipation, suspense, or surprise? Can you have a relationship without these? How does he experience what we see as the rolling out of destiny as it happens: Creation, Moses, World Wars I and II, the year 2021, and the year 3019? This blows my mind!

God Is outside of Time and Space.

I can't grasp this concept well enough to even create an if... then... statement.

God Made and Sustains Creation

If God's Creation is designed, intentional, complex, and interrelated, then it's much more than just us on this tiny planet orbiting in space. Surely there is some deeper purpose for the size of the universe. God seems to set everything up with a purpose. It seems there are likely some other forms of life somewhere out there. I'm in continual awe!

If God sustains his Creation, then without his presence and his holding everything together, we would cease to exist – stars, planets, and people – everything. At any point in time, at his command, we could cease to exist.

God Is Omnipresent

If God is present throughout this entire universe – not just everywhere on earth, then he is present in all. We can't escape his presence. He is always with us.

God Is All-Powerful

If God can change anything and everything at any time he pleases, even outside of time, then what does that mean about the power of choice he gave us?

Maybe his greatest display of power is in holding all things together and in sustaining them through the way he has designed them, including us. God seldom makes changes to his original design. He almost always allows natural laws to play out: gravity, seasons, days, and the very nature of life and death.

For living creatures who make choices, this also includes the law of reaping what we sow. He doesn't appear to take away the choice he provided to mankind and other creatures.

God Is Holy

If God is holy, "set apart," not one of us, then we are very different from him. We may be made in his image, but only in part. We possess a tiny bit of his creativity, ability, capacity, and power. We're quite limited.

Beliefs Tree

After I did the "If... then..." assessment, I developed a beliefs tree, similar to a decision tree. Using the tree analogy, the root system represents my strongest and deepest beliefs about life, those in which I have the most confidence. My additional beliefs spill from the trunk of the tree, then branch into several further beliefs.

I hoped this would help me better understand how my beliefs connected, or where there were gaps and discrepancies that needed to be resolved. I found this exercise to be helpful, yet it was also redundant of some of my other assessments. Even so, it was a good exercise and brought further clarity.

My deepest beliefs – the roots – are:
- Humans are limited.
- We use our minds to try to determine our beliefs and live our lives.

These are my secondary beliefs – the main branches:
- We feel and act based on what we think.
- Mentally, emotionally, and developmentally, we are where we think we are, not necessarily where we really are. It's our thinking that determines whether we are in a good place, a bad place, in God's presence or not, and so on.
- We are always in the presence of our Creator, and no place is good or bad. We make our environment what we think it is in our minds.
- All spiritual beliefs are believed in faith. We can't prove or disprove God. We are all people of faith; we all believe things we have never seen.
- No one has full knowledge of God. We know only in part, and a small part at that.

- Most people don't think much about God or our existence. We live heads-down, focused on ourselves, family, and the earth. We've probably done this for all of human history. What does our lack of attention mean to God? What does he think and feel about us – our successes; our failures; our learnings; our experiences; our striving to be good, loving, caring stewards of ourselves and our families?
- What we believe about God and Creation impacts how we live our lives and how we process our experiences. We can see God as a judge, a genie, our servant, or our Father. We might feel that he is distant or intimate; loving and forgiving, or wrathful and punishing. We can even see him as nonexistent. We live based on what we see and feel, not necessarily on who he is.
- We see what we believe to be true, or what we would like to be true. This is evident in how we interpret everything: politics, spirituality, pleasure, dread, right and wrong, and cause and effects.
- We see things the way we are, not necessarily as they really are, and then we act based on our perspective and our faith in what will happen next if we do and if we don't.
- Everything was designed and created. It didn't happen by chance. God's design is massive, complex, detailed, and all interrelated. We never fully understand his design.

Each of these beliefs then birthed additional sub-beliefs, or smaller branches on my metaphorical tree. The exercise went six levels deep.

This exercise provided additional perspective, and the consistency was encouraging. It reflected how our individual thinking leads to our beliefs, which lead to our feelings and then ultimately to our actions.

We're quite limited in our ability to think and process Creation and God. We do our best based on our level of interest, concern, and focus.

The Pyramid View

I also looked at my beliefs from a top down, pyramid perspective. In this exercise I tried to tie my various assessments together into one summary document that would provide a big-picture perspective – a holistic view of where I'd been and what I'd concluded so far on my spiritual journey. I wanted to know what I believed and have more confidence in those beliefs.

My pyramid showed me that I have tried to understand my spiritual beliefs from many different perspectives that have all provided some more clarity and a lot more questions. I no longer feel that I can relate well spiritually to anyone, while at the same time my appreciation of God is growing. I feel like I'm on an island by myself.

As a result of the pyramid exercise, I formulated yet another list of my new or deeper perspectives (see the next section). This spiritual journey has been an exploration into unknown territory – a land foreign to anything my pre-concussion self ever expected to encounter. Discovering all I can about God and our existence has prompted me to see God as much more than I've ever viewed him in the past, and I see earth and mankind as only a small piece of his creation. Seeking God has led people down many different paths. It's incredible that our paths have been so different, as we are all seeking the same enlightenment. I don't have all the answers, or even many of them, but I'm thankful that I'm still seeking God. The pyramid gave me a more holistic view of what I had been trying to bring more clarity to – added perspective, but not necessarily any more answers. The good news is that this review didn't create many incremental questions about my beliefs; it simply summarized what I had already identified.

New or Deeper Perspectives

Interpreting Life's Challenges and Surprises

After learning what I could from these various assessments and documents, I wanted to better understand how I should process and deal with challenges, especially when interacting with others. These included some upsetting events that happened to my family and friends. Here are some of the heart-wrenching situations I was facing:

- My nephew's death as a young adult
- A friend's motorcycle accident
- Several women in our family testing positive for genetic cancer risk
- Our daughter's challenges as a gym-owner

I continue to worship God. I focus on him and his Creation! I try to put such events into perspective relative to Creation. I acknowledge that God has allowed them to happen. He knew about them before they happened. He knew about them during his original design. For my family and I, the consequences of everyone's choices and actions have compounded, which is his natural law.

As I thought before my concussion, I found that I still think it's best to focus on what I control. I also love to encourage others to push through and see the big, big picture. This seems to be the best way to deal with the hard times. (I share much more about this concept in my book *How to Refocus Your Life*.)

Hope

Hope is trusting in God's design and timing. This is in contrast to hoping for a radical change, which would require God to override his original, perfect design. In my experience, God doesn't often interfere with his original design. Everything unfolds, whether or not we like it or understand it, in his perfect timing, which is known by God beforehand.

What remains is that I should be an encourager, sharing my love and heart, feeling the weight of others' experiences, hurting with them, and helping them. My priorities are living compassionately and helping others feel remembered and that they matter.

I continue to intentionally change and grow – my thinking drives my actions and feelings. I can work toward creating a better future by focusing on possibilities instead of limitations. I hope to be an excellent steward and control what is in my control!

Different Religions

There are many interpretations of God, whether through books or religions. We each see him differently in regard to his character and what he wants.

No Interpretation Is Fully Correct

No interpretation of Scripture or God is fully correct and completely understood by any of us. And yet some elements seem pretty easy for many of us to understand. Some people, convinced they know the truth, share their ideas freely with everyone, in integrity and sincerity, and with conviction. What seems true to one person is likely not the whole truth, yet some of us try to convince others, even with our limited understanding of God, in hopes they will come to believe as we do. Our motives are often pure, and we often share our hearts with sincerity, but I'm not confident that what we share is ever the whole truth.

If we know we don't understand the whole truth, when is it appropriate to share our spiritual beliefs with others? It would seem to be appropriate when the other person is demonstrating interest and is asking us for our perspective, but now that I have questions about so many spiritual values, pushing my beliefs on others feels wrong, especially since I'm convinced I don't understand the whole truth. It's hard to accept that I will never fully understand much of the magnitude and scope of God.

The Day-to-Day

It's easy to focus only on what is in front of us, living life on autopilot and going through the motions. Many people don't think of the bigger picture and the presence of a Creator or God during their day-to-day activities. When we focus on our urgent needs and instant gratification, we can miss the enormity of the big picture. I wonder how God feels about that focus. If we are being good stewards of what he has given us, maybe he's pleased.

I believe God loves for us to have a relationship with him, or at least an appreciation of what he designed and created. I believe he loves when I sit and admire him and his Creation.

I've tried to seek greater clarity about God in a variety of ways. They have each been helpful in their own way, and my questions continue to grow. They continue to overwhelm me, tempting me to quit my pursuit of spiritual truth, but I know that's not the right thing to do. So I will continue to seek more clarity and deal with my new questions as they come.

Chapter 9

The Bible and Jesus

My primary source for learning spiritual beliefs has been the Bible. As I've taken a deeper look into the Bible, I've gained some clarity but also a lot more questions. I believed the Bible came directly from God, but I feel less confident about that now.

I'm hesitant and fearful as I document my uncertainties regarding what the Bible says about Jesus. I continually stop as I think and write, asking myself, "What am I doing?" But these are honest questions.

The Bible is based on writings from several authors who reported what I've believed to be the truth. I was curious about what the New Testament writers – Jesus's eyewitnesses – said in quoting Jesus, in contrast to what they wrote from their own points of view. Although inspired by God, they were still fully human. Jesus is described as fully human and yet fully God.

Jesus's Early Life

It's disappointing to me that none of the New Testament was written by Jesus, but instead was written by those who knew him after he began his three-year ministry at age 30. I would like to have seen what he personally wrote, but we don't have that option. The only writing by Jesus that I'm aware of is when he bent down and wrote in the dirt when he was talking to the accusers of the woman who was caught in adultery. Everything in the New Testament was written by someone else, and this writing began about 30 years after he died and was risen, and much was written well after that.

None of the writings of the New Testament were written by someone who knew him during his first 30 years of life, except perhaps the book of James. James was probably Jesus's half-brother, and even he didn't write about Jesus as a young person. There aren't books written by his father, Joseph, or his mother, Mary. It seems peculiar to me that, being God, he didn't reveal much during his first 30 years of life, at least based on the writings we have. There is one short passage about his being a young man teaching at a temple, but that's all that's shared. It's like a switch was suddenly flipped on when he turned 30. How could he possibly hide the fact that he was God, or God's Son? Wouldn't it continually spill out of his life in everything he did?

As a writer I know how hard it is to accurately recall information in detail – and with the emotion it carried – from an experience that occurred even the previous day. When I don't complete my daily journal until the following morning, much has been lost. This personal experience makes me wonder about the accuracy of documentation that occurred more than 30 years after Jesus's life. It's what we have available, and the content is excellent, but I'm disappointed that my spiritual beliefs are based on documentation that took place so long after the original events.

What Jesus Said According to John

I've never had questions regarding who Jesus was. He just was. It makes me feel uncomfortable that I now have questions about who he was, even though they're logical questions. I continue to tell myself, *God is truth, and he can handle my asking honest, heart-based questions.* My questions come from a loving, open heart and mind, and I'm certain they don't rattle him. I think he's pleased I'm being even more honest and open with him. He's hearing me acknowledge things he has known all along. I'm the one getting rattled, as I think through and verbalize these thoughts.

To better understand what Jesus was recorded to have said and taught in the book of John, the apostle, I created a table listing his sayings in John, and how many times each is documented. I focused on what Jesus said about himself. Here's what I found:

Jesus is from heaven.

I found four places where Jesus stated that he came down from heaven, or from God.

Jesus was sent by God.

I counted at least 26 places in the book of John where Jesus stated he was sent by God.

Jesus is one with God.

Jesus believed and taught that he was one with God, stating, "The Father and I are one" and "If you have seen me, you have seen the Father." This is the closest to Jesus saying "I am God" that I found in the book of John.

God is Jesus's father.

Jesus called God his father at least 22 times. At that time, I understand from the teachings of the Jewish leaders, it wasn't acceptable for anyone to call God their father. His claim was much different from what we think when we say we're all God's children or God is the father of us all. This was a dramatic and bold claim. He was definitely saying that he was related to God in a direct way, differently from anyone else. This is perplexing because he stated both that he was God and that God was his father. This is still a mystery.

For years people have tried to better understand what is referred to as the Trinity – one God and yet three: Father, Son, and Holy Spirit. I'm not going to solve this one. This is a mystery too.

Twenty-four times Jesus referred to God as "my Father." This is in addition to the times he called God "Father." Sometimes his "my Father" comments are linked to statements that his father is also God. The other times it is inferred. He spoke about "the Father" 40 additional times without explicitly saying "my Father."

Multiple times he stated, "The Father and I are one" or "The Father is in me and I am in the Father." But he also stated, "The Father is greater than I am." These are hard conundrums to process. This is probably one of the reasons it's so hard to understand or comprehend the concept of the Trinity.

According to John, Jesus believed God was his father, and yet they were one and they were in each other, and yet "the Father" was somehow greater than Jesus.

Jesus is God's Son or the Son of God.

Nineteen times John reported Jesus calling himself "God's Son" or the "Son of God." And there are seven places in John where others, including John himself, John the Baptist, and Martha, referred to Jesus as the "Son of God."

Jesus is the Messiah.

Four times Jesus referred to himself as "the Messiah." Four other people also stated that they believed Jesus was the Messiah. Jesus said he was the savior of the world, and also that he was the one who provided life after death and the ability to never die. Jesus stated he was the stairway between heaven and earth, that he came down from heaven, that if you believe in him you will have eternal life, that he will raise believers up on the last day, and that believers will not die but will live forever. Several of these statements are hard to comprehend and believe with our limited minds and understanding.

Jesus will be raised from the dead.

In John 14, Jesus predicted he would be raised from the dead to live again. He was forecasting the future knowing what was coming. Based on Scripture, he was correct.

Jesus is the way, the truth, and the life.

In John 14:6 Jesus stated:

> *I am the way, the truth, and the life. No one can come to the Father except through me. If you had really known me, you would know who my Father is. From now on, you do know him and have seen him!*

From this passage we learn that Jesus believed the only way to get to God was through himself. There were no other options. I think this is one of the reasons some find Jesus so hard to believe. It leads people to either believe this statement, believe that he's a liar, or believe that he was deceived regarding who he was. *He* didn't seem confused; he was confident in who he was and in his knowledge of God. For at least the past 55 years, I believed he was telling the truth and that he is God, or the Son of God, or both.

His bold statement, "If you had really known me, you would know who my Father is," is hard to comprehend, but means he is the Father, or is the same as the Father, or is such a reflection of the Father that they are inseparable.

I still believe all these things about Jesus, but not with the same level of confidence when I consider the documentation my beliefs are based on. My belief was more automatic in the past. To get there now, I'm making a choice to believe it.

Jesus provides eternal life.

Jesus said 10 times that he provides eternal life to people. He also stated they will never die, and that he saves them. Some metaphors or descriptions in Scripture for receiving this gift are: drinking the living water he provides, believing in him, eating the bread that comes from heaven, eating his flesh and drinking his blood, feeding on him, obeying his teachings, coming in through him as a gate, following him, and following the commands of "the One" who sent him.

He clearly stated that we can live forever, not die, and be saved through him. It's not a simple, easy-to-understand formula. These are bold, sometimes difficult statements to understand.

Jesus is all-knowing.

At least four times in John, Jesus revealed that he knew things that had been hidden in the past, or knew them before they happened. He did this with Nathanael, saying he saw Nathanael ahead of their introduction; with an adulterous woman at a well, revealing that she had been with six men; with Judas, who would betray him; and with Peter, who would deny he knew Jesus within 24 hours. Based on these few examples it appears Jesus knew more than the common man regarding someone's past and future actions. Based on what John observed, there were at least a few times when Jesus knew things others didn't, in a God-like way. This is consistent with other statements in Scripture, including the other Gospels, which reflects that Jesus was all-knowing, or at least more knowing, if these were cases in which God provided revelation to him.

Jesus is Teacher and Lord.

In John 13:13, when Jesus was washing the feet of his disciples, as a lesson to them he said:

You call me "Teacher" and "Lord," and you are right, because that's what I am.

Some believe Jesus was a great teacher who taught many helpful life concepts. If he taught both truth and some falsehood, how would you know which parts were true and which were false? If what he taught isn't all true, such as being the only way to God, that he came from God, and that he's one with God – then maybe we wouldn't see him as a great teacher. He'd be considered a liar. It would make it harder to listen to him if you needed to separate truth and wisdom from dishonesty and deceit. Can you trust the words of a person who doesn't always tell the truth, or do you run, not wanting to be associated with them?

I haven't understood or believed all the teachings of anyone I've seen, heard, or read about. I highly value some or much of what they share or teach, and disregard other things that don't align with my beliefs and experiences. This is true about even the teachers I most respect: John Wooden, John C. Maxwell, and the others I wrote about in chapter 4. I'm guessing you do the same. Should we behave differently in regard to Jesus's teachings? Another question for which I don't have the answer.

This is what makes Scripture challenging for some. This question has weighed on my mind now for a few years. Based on what I see today, should I believe Jesus is God? At the same time, based on my first 61 years of life and all the biblical teaching and experiences I've had, how can I not believe he's God? This paradox feels like a ton of bricks on my back, and I've not yet been able to reconcile it or shake it.

Jesus is a miracle-worker and healer.

Seven times in John, Jesus is cited as specifically healing someone or working a miracle. This includes healing sick people, raising a dead man, walking on water, and healing eyes. This of course opens up the controversial topic of believing in miracles. Some Christians do and others don't. I have not personally seen a miracle, but I believe they have or can exist. I'm confused about when God provides them.

You can ask for anything.

Jesus also stated, "You can ask me for anything in my name and I will do it!" I've asked many times, and in various ways, for God to provide something that didn't happen the way I hoped and asked for it to occur. I've heard plenty of messages of encouragement about how to take these results, but they don't feel right. They include "It's not the time for it yet," "The answer from God must be no," and "The person you asked to have healed was healed because they died and were delivered from their pain," which wasn't what I asked of God. What did Jesus mean when he said to ask for anything?

One interpretation of the "ask for anything" statement is that Jesus was speaking to only one particular person or group that he was with at the time. Maybe it was never intended as a promise to all of us in the future, or something we should take to heart and try to apply to our lives. In my Christian culture, most believe that anything stated in Scripture applies to or works for anyone who trusts in God. I haven't found that to be true. I'm leaning more toward believing that Jesus did say these things, he did mean them, and that they were true, but maybe only for the specific people who were present at the time he said them.

To better explain this, if I'm out with a friend for a meal and I offer to pay for their meal, that doesn't mean any person can apply what I said to themselves, expecting to get a free meal anywhere, at any time, because they heard me say this to one person. Maybe we shouldn't try to extrapolate from his statements to create our own "genie" who will provide what we want.

But Jesus duplicated this claim with these statements:

If you remain in me and my words remain in you, you may ask for anything you want, and it will be granted!

I appointed you to go and produce lasting fruit, so the Father will give you whatever you ask for, using my name.

These are challenging as well, and I haven't seen or experienced them in my life.

John's Statements about Jesus

John, as a disciple of Jesus's teaching for about three years, made some bold statements. Early in the book of John he made several statements about "the Word." From the verses that follow those statements, it appears *the Word* refers to Jesus. But John didn't say, "Jesus is the Word"; he said:

In the beginning the Word already existed. The Word was with God, and the Word was God. He existed in the beginning with God.

He also said, "God created everything through the Word," which I assume is Jesus. Then, "Nothing was created except through him." A few verses later he said, "So the Word became human and made his home among us." He also said, "He came into the very world he created." If Jesus is the Word, then Jesus created everything and put himself into this tiny little part of his Creation. Again, I've believed this based on what John said. I now clearly acknowledge it's not necessarily based on what Jesus said. This doesn't make it true or untrue, but it clarifies for me the origin of what Jesus has been documented as saying.

Twice in the book of John, John the Baptist referred to Jesus as the "Lamb of God." I didn't find anywhere where Jesus called himself by that title.

There are examples in John of Jesus having standard, human traits. John referred to Jesus's weeping over the death of a friend, and being weary at a well. In Hebrews it says he was tempted in every way just like us. These descriptions of Jesus confirm he was a man with human traits and experiences.

Other Statements about Jesus

In Matthew 3 it appears that John the Baptist, who was Jesus's cousin, didn't know Jesus was the chosen one until he baptized Jesus when Jesus was believed to be 30 years old. It surprises me that John the Baptist didn't know his own cousin was the Son of God until that time, though they might have lived miles apart, and we know Jesus's parents traveled and lived in different places. But in Luke 1:39–42, Mary, Jesus's mother, and Elizabeth, John's mother, knew one another:

> *A few days later Mary hurried to the hill country of Judea, to the town where Zechariah lived. She entered the house and greeted Elizabeth. At the sound of Mary's greeting, Elizabeth's child leaped within her, and Elizabeth was filled with the Holy Spirit. Elizabeth gave a glad cry and exclaimed to*

Mary, "God has blessed you above all women, and your child is blessed."

The mothers had some relationship and interacted with each other. We don't know about the relationship between John and Jesus prior to the time of Jesus's baptism, but it would surprise me if they didn't know each other to some degree or didn't know about each other, especially from a spiritual perspective, due to what was shared between Mary and Elizabeth during that visit.

It's even harder to comprehend how Jesus's own brothers didn't believe he was the Son of God, as it states in John 7. How could he be the Son of God, and hide that for 30 years so that even his own brothers didn't believe it? In Philippians 2:7–8 it says:

Instead, he gave up his divine privileges; he took the humble position of a slave and was born as a human being. When he appeared in human form, he humbled himself in obedience to God and died a criminal's death on a cross.

What does "gave up his divine privileges" mean? Other versions state that he "emptied himself." How much of God was he on the earth? What did he give up and what did he still have? I'm not sure that we really know. We understand that he lived a perfect, sinless life; that he knew some things about the past and the future; and that he performed some miracles. What other characteristics of God were a part of his life? Wouldn't living perfectly throughout his entire life somehow stand out to everyone around him? If my brother or sister lived a perfect life during their first 30 years, I think it would have been very apparent to me, at least in contrast to me and my other non-perfect sibling. The standard of perfect is far above anything I have lived or been exposed to. How could it not stand out?

Jesus might have been fully human, as defined by Scripture, but at age 30 he began to display some of his God powers through the miracles he performed. How could his being God be hidden and not be reflected and revealed in his day-to-day life, convincing his own brothers? Did he not seem different in his thoughts, words, and actions? There might be a good explanation, but I can't comprehend it any better than I can comprehend the size and content of our universe.

Religious Leaders

I'm curious about the Jewish leaders described in the Bible – the Pharisees and the Sadducees. Based on Jesus's comments, these religious leaders all seemed to be in the wrong. Jesus made some strong global statements about these groups. If they were truly seeking God, wouldn't at least some of them have seen Jesus as God, or at least as the Son of God? How did they miss him? That would be like a police department of 500, all wearing badges, and not one of them really trying to uphold the truth or protect the public. Is that what the Pharisees and Sadducees were like?

The Bible cites some priests, in the book of Acts, after Jesus had died and been raised again, who saw him as God. But while Jesus was physically on earth, some of these religious leaders who studied the Old Testament surely should have found God in Jesus. It's hard to comprehend that Jesus didn't convince them he was God. Or perhaps they were not truly seeking God. Were they just playing the role that they had been given? Surely some of them wanted to know God, and please him. How could they be so wrong in their searching?

Who Was Jesus?

The books of Matthew, Mark, Luke, and John are our primary sources for what was said of Jesus. He was a remarkable and wise man who lived on this tiny planet over 2,000 years ago and may have been the Son of God and/or God himself; or he was a teacher who was either deceived or crazy, or who intentionally deceived his followers about his nature.

Those who seek knowledge of Jesus can choose what to believe about him. Though I have more questions than ever, I still choose to believe that Jesus was the person represented in the Gospels. This takes a more conscious act of faith on my part than in the past. This is my choice.

The Bible, or parts of it, has positively impacted many lives over the past 2,000 years, and especially over the past four to six hundred years. It has been a core foundation of my life for 55 years. But as you can see, I haven't yet found answers to my questions about Jesus as portrayed in the Bible.

Chapter 10

Knowing God and Christianity

My questions might seem bold, surprising, or maybe even alarming. I'm being deeply transparent and honest about them. My thinking and understanding about my spiritual beliefs is now much more gray than simply black and white.

How much do we seek to know God? How many of us seek him? How many of us care whether there is or isn't a God? When we seek him, does it feel safe, or scary? And how much of him can we really comprehend? Does seeking God lead to more answers or more questions?

Sometimes a difficult personal challenge drives us to seek help from a source beyond ourselves. But that motivation can mean that the attempt is self-serving and not a sincere effort to get to know God. Most people are focused on the here and now. With the focus on what is right before us, the existence of a God, a Creator, or even a divine universe can be way beyond anything we pursue.

I personally want to know where we came from and who our Creator is. When we seek truth, we seem to discover many different results, both across religions and within religions. The result might be that we call God something different, describe his characteristics differently, or feel called to live differently in our practices and routines.

If there is one true God and Creator, how can we perceive him so differently? Is that by design? Is that the way he intended it? It must be; he knew we would respond this way when he designed us. This too boggles my mind, and challenges my beliefs. I will continue to pursue the truth about God, and try the best I can to learn more about him, while remaining in awe of him and his wonderful universe.

Based on our humanness and our limited minds – in contrast to my past confidence that we can know God well – I believe nobody can really know God well, or as well as they think they do. I'm convinced some of us do know God in part, but in only a very little part. We were not designed to have the capacity to know him well or comprehend much of him. We have, at best, glimpses from our own perspective, but we still should pursue knowledge of him through Scripture, knowing it's only a tiny part of who he is. We're limited by time and space. We can't begin to imagine beyond the time and space of our existence on earth.

Many believe Jesus revealed God to us. And though Jesus's descriptions are difficult to fully understand, we can know much about God from Jesus's perspective.

It's hard for me to listen to people who "know" they have the answers to everything. I'm not convinced any of us do. When someone says they know the truth, it seems to me they're playing God. I get cautious and a bit defensive when I hear this, and I find myself much less open to what they say. I try to listen, but I'm skeptical about what they have to say. Their quick, pat answers don't seem to reveal truth. I think the truth is grayer and more complex.

There's nothing wrong with sharing our beliefs and stating them as such, but to state that a belief is the truth seems inconsistent with the limited capacity of our minds.

If I had been born in a different family, in another part of the world, or into a different religion, wouldn't my beliefs be different from what they are? It's like being told Coke is the best soda and yet never having been given the chance to taste Pepsi, Sprite, Mountain Dew, or Dad's Root Beer. I wouldn't know which was the best; I would have to be given the opportunity to try those other products before knowing the truth.

It's shocking to me that I'm objectively questioning what was formerly "true" for me and stating my new reservations openly for the first time. Up to age 61, I'd never objectively selected Christianity as my spiritual belief; it was simply the default option that seemed right. It still feels right, but I wonder if it's the whole picture, or complete, or if it's missing some vital aspects of God and his Creation that I have not been exposed to.

It would be much easier to sweep these broader and deeper thoughts under the carpet and act like they don't exist, but I'm no longer willing to do that, or at least not at this point in my spiritual journey. I would rather explore these questions and learn from them to become a deeper, more mature person – more honest and real than I've ever been. It's interesting that my desire to go deeper and face many tougher questions has occurred since my concussion. I'm not sure why.

When I discuss Christianity with others, I sometimes feel like I'm on a different planet. As a life coach, I believe we each live in our own unique world, because no one else has seen and experienced the exact same things we have, in the same order, in the same way, or from the same people. I seem to have core assumptions, priorities, dreams, and desires that are different from those of many others, even those close to me. I want to think about different things, see different things, listen to and watch different things, hear different sound levels, and spend more quiet, isolated times away to think than others do. I truly feel different from most other people.

Perhaps we all experience feeling different from everyone else. If that's the case, maybe one of our common traits is that we all feel unique. One of the potential benefits of publishing *Turning Gray* is for me to connect with others who feel the same way. Maybe I'm not as isolated as I think I am. If you find yourself feeling estranged like this, I hope you'll reach out to me. I would like you to know that you're not alone.

Sometimes I feel isolated because I'm diving into deep, uncharted spiritual waters and facing my questions and uncertainty, and one of my biggest fears is the impacts on my relationships with others. I fear I won't be loved and accepted by those who have loved and accepted me in the past. Our spiritual commonalities have bound us together in the past, and now that my spiritual perspective is shifting, I hope I won't lose that love and acceptance.

Even if I've not yet landed on my revised beliefs, I wonder if I will I be treated differently by those I care about. I don't want to be left out, alone, by myself, but I feel like I'm locked in a cage with my thoughts and feelings. I don't even know if I should get out, but I want to be in sync with others. It's quite confusing. And I feel like I've been here for a long time; feelings of isolation can really slow down the passage of time.

Many More Questions

Chapter 11

Questions – The Bible

Over the past three years I've had quite a few questions concerning the Bible that I've never put on paper. Maybe I've been too afraid to do so due to my sacred respect for the Bible.

Origins of the Bible

I was taught from Scripture, both the Old Testament and the New Testament. I was taught the names of the books, the order of the books, overviews and themes, and some details, but never where the Bible came from or how it came to be – just that it came from God through trustworthy men.

I see the Bible as God's Word – a message from him, but through others. I have valued its insights, direction, and perspectives. But is the Bible truly from God if it was written by sinful people? What criteria allow us to judge it as *the* source, *the* truth? Why should we trust the people who had the authority to decide what would and wouldn't be included?

Why was it written so long after the events – Creation, Jesus's time on earth, and so on? A lot of core teachings were recorded well after Jesus's time on earth, like the letters and teachings of Paul, Peter, James, and John. What made Moses, Matthew, Mark, Luke, John, Paul, Peter, and others so special? Why do we believe that only they heard the definitive words of God?

Why did the collection of New Testament books we use today come together 5,600 years or more into our 6,000-plus-year existence? Some biblical reference materials project that Creation began approximately 6,000 years ago, not millions of years ago. If this timing is generally correct, then our current New Testament has been widely available in this format for only 7 percent or less of our time on earth.

How can the Bible be God's intentional message considering how it came together over many, many years and through various politically motivated influencers?

The Bible was the center of my family members' beliefs. It was almost like a copy of the Bible had been handed down from God to Adam and Eve, and they had a copy of it in their home. My simplistic view was that the Bible had always been here, intact and available for all time. I wasn't taught at church that it has been available from the time of Adam and Eve; it just seemed that it had been. I now realize I was wrong and that it was written by men long after Jesus lived.

It felt wrong to start to question the Bible as God's Word for our lives. Even ordering books on the topic made me feel I was betraying my faith. I wondered if it was okay to question its origins. I crossed that line in my mind, and have been fortunate to profit from the insights I have gained.

Evaluating the truth of the Bible is surely a standard part of the education for a seminary student, and others have shared that it was a part of their basic Christian education, but it feels very foreign to me to do this.

The King James Version of the Bible that I grew up with hasn't been on earth or in the hands of commoners for very long relative to the biblical timeline of Creation. What I considered the source of teachings that have always directed mankind has been available only since 1611.

The Old Testament contains the sacred scriptures of the Jewish faith, written at different times between about 1200 and 165 BC. The New Testament was written by Christians in the first century AD. According to History.com, the Muratorian Canon, which is believed to date to 200 AD, is the earliest compilation of canonical texts resembling the New Testament. It was not until the fourth or fifth century that Christian churches came to a basic agreement on biblical canon.

The Bible has traditionally been taught by the leaders of a congregation. At the time of the Reformation, in the sixteenth century, people like Martin Luther translated the Scriptures so that the general population could have access to it. More literacy and an increase in the availability of printing presses had a great deal to do with making the Bible more accessible to the general public. A printed Bible in a common language is a relatively new resource for clearly understanding how we are to live. That doesn't make it invalid, but it's a big shift from the image of the Bible that I grew up with. I believed it was the source of our faith because it had always been there. My perspective is now informed by history.

We naturally think that something that has been with us since we can first remember was always there. We can acknowledge that at one point it didn't exist, but emotionally it's hard to imagine a different, earlier life. Books, movies, and television give us a sense of what life might have been like in the past, but we of course can't know what the experience was really like.

My life has always included cars, planes, phones, radios, televisions, refrigerators, and mass-production books, but my grandparents lived through the introductions of these conveniences. For some of you, inventions that occurred during my life have existed for all of yours: microwave ovens, cell phones, computers, rolling suitcases, and so much more.

I ordered three books written by Christian authors about the origins of the Bible. I haven't ventured to read a non-Christian's perspective, but I gained a lot of knowledge from these few Christian-authored books:

- *How We Got the Bible* by Timothy Paul Jones, PhD
- *How We Got the Bible: A Visual Journey* by Clinton E. Arnold
- *The Origin of the Bible* by F. F. Bruce, J. I. Packer, Philip Comfort, and Carl F. H. Henry (I'm still slowly reading this longer book)

These books convey how much effort has been spent to stay true to the original documents, which have been discovered over the years. They also share how much effort has been taken to translate the Bible into various languages, how passages were evaluated and selected (or not selected) for inclusion, that being an eyewitness was a significant criterion for whether or not someone's writing was included, and that the focus was always on Jesus being central to the message. They provided more insight than I had been taught, or at least more than I remember. They answered some of my questions but also created more.

More Questions about the Bible

- Why did Jesus not write down some of his teachings or have someone else write them down? We only have what others heard and remembered.

- Why were the Gospels not written until 30 years and longer after Jesus's death? That is a long time to keep facts straight when you don't have paper and pen sitting around, a PC to type into, or photos to jog your memory. I have trouble writing about things that happened a few years ago, and that's with the help of my notes, photos, files, and recordings.

The authors of the Bible didn't have these conveniences. They relied on the spoken word to keep the facts straight for those 30-plus years. I can hardly imagine how the facts could remain accurate for that long – and for longer in the case of other biblical writings. I think of the game Telephone, and what people refer to as tall stories. I hope the stories and teachings in the Bible are indeed factual and accurate, but I now wonder about it.

- Being an eyewitness to Jesus's ministry sounds like a good requirement for qualifying as a valid recorder of Scripture, but that doesn't ensure that that person has an excellent memory or that they can accurately document what happened and when it happened 30 to 60 years later.

- Who has the authority to decide who is hearing from God and who is not? That feels subjective. There were numerous eyewitnesses to Jesus's life and teachings whose recollections aren't recorded in the bible, so why weren't more of them included?

Why are Peter, John, Paul, and others (including Moses and the prophets of the Old Testament) given so much credibility? Who selected their writings over those of others to be included in the Bible? Who decided they had heard from God in ways that others hadn't, and that they were able to relay the information accurately and without bias? We often believe the words of leaders of movements without questioning them. When someone is raised up as the leader of a group, we assume what they say is credible. Think of George Washington, Abraham Lincoln, Mahatma Gandhi, Martin Luther King Junior, and many others. The writers of the Gospels were clearly the Christian leaders of the time.

I know it's said that being an author grants you credibility no matter what you know or what you've done. Maybe the apostles and others gained credibility simply because they had the skill and took the time to write, or had the resources to have someone else document their thoughts and words.

- Some Scripture was written or documented by people who weren't present during the events they recorded. Moses described Creation, but was not around when it occurred – no one was. He also wrote about Abraham, Isaac, Jacob, Hagar, Bilhah, and many others he couldn't have known. Was he given this information by God or did he interview people who had either been present at these events or spoke to participants who were once, twice, or three times removed from the events? The level of detail that's documented, without citing sources, including people's emotions and intentions, creates questions in my mind as to its authenticity.

Are these just stories to make a point, and whether they're true or not is irrelevant? Most of the stories are stated as fact rather than as "I saw… " "I heard…" "Someone told me…" or even "I heard from Bob that this happened and this is his account." They read like fictional stories; like the authors decided what to write about and what message they would convey. Yet the same events were documented by many different people at many different times in many different places, whether the authors were there or not.

How confident can we be in the accuracy of details about the Creation and the Old Testament when these happened so long ago and there isn't any contemporary documentation? The details provided in the early books of the Old Testament are without benefit of the support systems and tools I mentioned earlier, like photographs, computers, and easily available pen and paper. They can be true, and from God, but for the first time they're harder for me to believe.

- Why did God not provide our Bible and its key messages earlier in our years on earth? Portions of the Old Testament existed hundreds of years before Jesus came to earth, but not the whole as we know it today. The New Testament experiences could not have been documented until they occurred, which was thousands of years into our time on earth, but was it his plan from the beginning to withhold this content from millions of lives for thousands of years?

  The Bible was defined for me as the guide for our lives. It provides us with the knowledge of God, and yet it has only been available in its current form, and to the common man, for about 10 percent or less of our 6,000-plus years on earth. I try to believe this was God's design, but it's hard!

- Kings have dictated that certain segments of the Bible be interpreted in certain ways by clergy when teaching the people. Some people have died trying to make the Bible available to the common man. Is that part of God's timing and plan? If not, and if God is all-knowing, he knew it would happen.

- I don't see a strong theme of love in the Old Testament. There are statements about God loving us, but most of them are general and global statements, particularly about his primarily caring for and protecting his people, not all the people of the world he created.

  Love surfaced strongly with Jesus in the New Testament. Why would the teachings of the first 4,000 years of mankind on earth not contain as much about love, especially when it became the primary theme of the New Testament? This seems inconsistent. Is it God's design?

- The Bible doesn't provide as much context for, or focus on, the act of Creation as I would hope or it seems like it should. The account we have was written more than 3,000 years after it occurred. Did God feel that additional detail about Creation was not necessary for humans to know, or that we couldn't understand the details?

Two Images at Once

My perspective of Scripture is like the optical-illusion drawing of an old woman and a young woman. They can both be seen in the same drawing, but people typically see only one or the other at first. If they try hard, eventually they might be able to see each image. I used to see only the image of Scripture in which it is unquestionably truth, and now I'm only seeing the other: the human elements of its development and content and the apparent inconsistencies. The harder I concentrate, the more distinctly I see the new image; I can't get the past image to reappear. It's frustrating and exhausting. I know the first image is still there, but I can't see it anymore. I have to accept the truth of Scripture on faith because I now wonder if the Bible is fully God's Word.

The Bible's Focus

With the landscape of the entire universe having been part of God's design and plan, it's hard for me to focus primarily on me, us, or our city, state, country, continent, or even planet, as many Christians do and as much of the Bible does. These are tiny in the scheme of Creation.

Reading the Bible now often seems self-focused and out of context to me. As intentional as God seems to be with every detail of his design, there must be more than just us and here, otherwise he wouldn't have created all of the stars and planets that we can't even see with our naked eye. I can't get my head around the idea that everything was exclusively created for human beings. It feels like there must be much more to Creation, and we're simply unaware of the magnitude and scope of it all. I have tried to tell myself to focus on the fact that Scripture is a message to mankind about just our portion of the big picture, but inside I still deeply desire to see and learn about so much more of Creation.

I've shared with Carolyn and others that I can't seem to get to earth. When I consider Creation, I can't regard the earth as being any more important to God than the other planets and the stars and galaxies. We seem important and of value, but not necessarily of any more value than any of the rest of God's Creation. It's like the planet Mercury; it's there, at least that's what I'm told, but I can't see it with my eyes because of the overwhelming, blinding brightness of the sun that drowns out anything in its vicinity. If God is intentional and purposeful about everything he has created, then even those things in the sky that we can see only through a powerful telescope must be there for a specific reason.

This nit of a nit of a nit of a nit of a place (our earth) can't be the center of everything. Even our galaxy is like a speck of dust in relation to the billions of trillions of stars in the universe. Compared to the Milky Way, our solar system is like a speck. And our planet is like a speck in relation to the solar system.

When I consider Ohio in relation to the earth, it appears as a speck. Columbus is a speck compared to Ohio. And I seem like a speck compared to Columbus. I am a speck of a speck of a speck of a speck of a speck of a speck of dust. Humans aren't much in relation to the total picture of Creation.

To help me visualize this, I created a simple diagram listing some of the levels between God and mankind:

By Faith	God Our Universe Our Galaxies
Only See A Glimpse	Stars The Sun and Our Solar System Earth America The United States
See With My Own Eyes	Ohio Columbus Westerville Our Neighborhood My Family Me

This was helpful, but didn't include much context. My next effort better reflects how small I am in God's scheme of the universe:

By Faith	# God	
	## Our Universe	
	### Our Galaxies	
Only See A Glimpse	Stars	
	The Sun and Our Solar System	
	Earth	
	America	
	The United States	
See With My Own Eyes	*Me*	

This diagram falls dramatically short of reality. The word *God* wouldn't come anywhere near fitting on this page, or even at the scale of our earth, and I would be smaller than a molecule. But it provides a quick visual reminder of how little I am in relation to God and Creation. You can barely see the *Earth*, and can't even read the *Me* at the bottom.

If I were convinced that the earth isn't the center of everything, I would warn everyone around me to broaden their perspective; but it's only my current viewpoint, not necessarily the whole truth. I find it much harder to be in situations in which the primary spiritual focus is on the earth and mankind, as it often is at church. I often quickly leave those environments. I'm trying to deal with my own experiences and what feels natural and true to me, which might seem misguided to others. But I need to deal with where I am this day, and live tomorrow based on the insights I get at that time.

We need to make it through each day, which is plenty for many of us, but I don't think that should be the center of our spiritual focus and attention. I want to honor and respect God, be in awe of him, and be thankful for what he has done and what he continues to do as he sustains Creation. I am only a tiny piece.

My dependence on God is stronger than ever, but it's harder to interact with him personally and to share my current experience with him when I know he already knows more about it than I ever will. I'm living the life he has provided me, and he's observing what he knows will happen in, with, and to me, but it no longer feels like I'm experiencing this together *with* him. It feels like a waste of effort and communication.

The Bible must be from God, somehow, at least generally. I continue to read it at least weekly. It provides context, perspective, insight, wisdom, and knowledge of God, and I'm confident it will continue to do so, but now perhaps through a different, or at least developing perspective.

I am forever thankful for the peace, direction, and lessons the Bible has provided and how it has changed me for the good. Yet I have a new uncertainty about its current role in my life. I still have tremendous respect for it, but I've lost confidence in it.

Chapter 12

Questions – Genesis

Genesis describes how people were created and how they lived on the earth for the first few thousand years. It provides some detail about certain key points of that stretch of time. I cover some of my new questions about Genesis in this chapter.

- What does it mean for God to "walk through the Garden of Eden"? My current belief is that he wasn't limited to a body until the Jesus part of him came to earth.

- Can a person hide from God in some way? From Genesis 3:9:

    Then the Lord God called to the man, "Where are you?"

    I understand a person wanting to hide from God, and trying to, but for God to ask this confuses me. Some say this was a rhetorical question, but that's not the way it reads to me. Not to mention that God appears to talk to Adam and Eve in a direct way, conveying clear messages that were understood in detail. How did God speak to them?

- From Genesis 3:21:

And the Lord God made clothing from animal skins for Adam and his wife.

I guess this is consistent with God creating everything else, but the phrase "made clothing" is quite different from his having "created" it. It's hard to comprehend God physically being on the earth and making clothes for Adam and Eve by killing animals for their skins (or creating animal skins).

- The serpent spoke to Adam and Eve using language they could understand. It would have to think and speak coherently in order to reason with them, and I'm not aware of any animals that have that capability.

  Maybe it wasn't the serpent that was talking, but rather Satan, who was embodying the serpent at that time. I'm not clear about Satan's existence, his form, or his capabilities, so except for the next two questions about the serpent/Satan, I'm leaving a clean slate in my mind with no assumptions about him for a later time in my journey.

- From Genesis 3:14:

  Then the Lord God said to the serpent, "Because you have done this, you are cursed more than all animals, domestic and wild. You will crawl on your belly, groveling in the dust as long as you live."

  Was the serpent somehow different before the curse, or does this verse infer that he would remain on the ground and not somehow eventually be able to walk? In the past I thought the serpent was literally a snake. Maybe it was and maybe it wasn't. I have believed that all snakes were cursed because of this statement by God. But now it seems to me that the statement was probably made specifically to that serpent, or Satan, and that all other snakes, by God's design, crawl on their bellies.

- I don't understand the biblical description of the timing of Satan on earth. Was he created as a serpent when the other animals were created? If so, how long did he live in that form? Is he still alive in that form today on the earth, or did he die as a serpent? How does that fit with other Scriptures that refer to Satan as alive and active today, and the Scripture in Isaiah 14:12–15 regarding his being a fallen angel? Isaiah prophesized about Satan:

    > *How you are fallen from heaven, O shining star, son of the morning! You have been thrown down to the earth, you who destroyed the nations of the world. For you said to yourself, "I will ascend to heaven and set my throne above God's stars. I will preside on the mountain of the gods far away in the north. I will climb to the highest heavens and be like the Most High." Instead, you will be brought down to the place of the dead, down to its lowest depths.*

    Was he an angel and fallen before Creation? If so, when was he given the physical serpent presence on earth? Was it on the fifth day, along with the other animals?

- In Genesis 3:22–24, God sounded surprised – not like an all-knowing God:

Then the Lord God said, "Look, the human beings have become like us, knowing both good and evil. What if they reach out, take fruit from the tree of life, and eat it? Then they will live forever!" So the Lord God banished them from the Garden of Eden, and he sent Adam out to cultivate the ground from which he had been made. After sending them out, the Lord God stationed mighty cherubim to the east of the Garden of Eden. And he placed a flaming sword that flashed back and forth to guard the way to the tree of life.

It sounds like God reacted to what he observed, like it was a surprise or new information. How could that be for an all-knowing God? Was he concerned that they would live forever? Why the concern? He created the tree of life and the tree of the knowledge of good and evil, and he knew they would eat of them or attempt to eat of them.

- When did the cherubim cease to be and go away? Why were they not mentioned later in the Scriptures? Wouldn't they still be here on earth? Why did he place the guard between the tree and Adam and Eve? What was it that he didn't want to happen, and why? Where is the tree today? Does it still exist somewhere? If not, when did it go away? How could a tree with that power exist for a time and then somehow cease to be? Did both the tree and the flaming swords protecting it get destroyed during the flood? Why don't they exist today?

- Wouldn't people have tried to find more ways to get access to the tree of life, to battle the angels or whatever it took? It seems it would have been a major focus for people through the ages to try to gain access to it. What changed that God would take it away?

- It also seems Adam and Eve must have already known the difference between good and evil on some level if they were tasked with making the decision to follow or not to follow God's command to not eat from the tree of the knowledge of good and evil. Otherwise they wouldn't have had a choice to make. If they didn't know the difference between good and evil, did they just take actions not knowing if they were good or evil? Not only would they not have known evil, they wouldn't have known what was good either. It seems they must have had some knowledge and criteria to help them decide whether or not to eat the forbidden fruit. Were people like animals in that they lived instinctively, not knowing any different – searching for food, eating, finding refuge, having sex, producing and raising offspring, exploring, soaring, and playing? Is that how we were before we knew the difference between good and evil? Did we make decisions based on some criteria provided by God? What were the criteria? Was it to obey God or not to obey God? Wouldn't the distinction still be good versus evil?

- Why did God reject Cain's sacrifice, or gift, in Genesis 4:2-5?:

Later she gave birth to his brother and named him Abel. When they grew up, Abel became a shepherd, while Cain cultivated the ground. When it was time for the harvest, Cain presented some of his crops as a gift to the Lord. Abel also brought a gift – the best portions of the firstborn lambs from his flock. The Lord accepted Abel and his gift, but he did not accept Cain and his gift. This made Cain very angry, and he looked dejected.

Wasn't taking care of the land and producing crops a reputable way to live and honor God? The only fact shared is that Cain cultivated the land. Was that evil? Why was his gift unacceptable to God? Since the writer decided to share that Cain was judged in this passage, why didn't he explain it better? Shouldn't there be a clear point to the fact that God did not look on his offering with favor? Is this story just a part of the backstory? Why was it included? What is the "right" that God asked Cain to do in verse 7:

You will be accepted if you do what is right. But if you refuse to do what is right, then watch out! Sin is crouching at the door, eager to control you. But you must subdue it and be its master.

- In Genesis 4:14, who did Cain fear would kill him – one of his brothers or sisters?:

    You have banished me from the land and from your presence; you have made me a homeless wanderer. Anyone who finds me will kill me!

Scripture describes Cain and Abel as the very first two brothers on earth; were there others alive at the time? Was this after many other brothers and sisters had been born, or even after several additional generations had been born? I have always assumed that it was early on in their life experiences, within their first 20 to 30 years of life; but maybe it occurred after they were much, much older. Scripture doesn't say, but the question does come to my mind.

- How did Cain leave God's presence in Genesis 4:16?:

    So Cain left the Lord's presence and settled in the land of Nod, east of Eden.

    How can any of us do that? Where is God not? Was he not also in the land of Nod? If God is only on or at certain places, where is he, and where isn't he? I have believed that God is omnipresent, everywhere, and holding all things together.

    After my initial response to this passage, I learned that the word translated as "presence" is the word for *face*. In Hebrew it carries the idea of someone's attention and blessing. Perhaps the passage means that he made a choice not to *follow* God. But he could not escape God's presence.

    It may be that many of my questions arise because I live in the year 2021 and have an English vocabulary and background. Maybe I must learn the meanings of the Hebrew words, and perhaps even the original languages the Scriptures were written in – Greek, Aramaic, etc. – to understand all of them correctly. It might take much more research, using footnotes, notations, and additional study aides, to understand what was intended. Scripture certainly is complex, and a simple English read of the text might not do it justice. I might have to depend on those who have studied the original text. This is discouraging when I think of others who are looking for answers as I am, especially new Bible readers.

- I also wonder how men and women in the Old Testament lived so long, and why some didn't have kids until they were quite old. I assume they were regularly having sex and using only natural birth control. It's possible that many births aren't recorded in the Scriptures, but in several cases parents had a firstborn when they were in their fifties, sixties, seventies, and eighties, and even later in the case of Abraham.

- Who were the Nephilites in Genesis 6:4?:

    In those days, and for some time after, giant Nephilites lived on the earth, for whenever the sons of God had intercourse with women, they gave birth to children who became the heroes and famous warriors of ancient times.

    Who were the "sons" of God? Why were their offspring giants, how did they become famous, and which ancient times did they live in?

- In Genesis 6, it sounds like God was frustrated that people are mortal flesh, evil, and wicked. He decided to reduce our lifespan to a mere 120 years versus the 700 to 900 years we had been living. From Genesis 6:1–3:

    Then the people began to multiply on the earth, and daughters were born to them. The sons of God saw the beautiful women and took any they wanted as their wives. Then the Lord said, "My Spirit will not put up with humans for such a long time, for they are only mortal flesh. In the future, their normal lifespan will be no more than 120 years."

Does God *discover* things about us? In verse 5 God noticed people were wicked, and in verses 6 and 7 this extended to all creatures:

The Lord observed the extent of human wickedness on the earth, and he saw that everything they thought or imagined was consistently and totally evil. So the Lord was sorry he had ever made them and put them on the earth. It broke his heart. And the Lord said, "I will wipe this human race I have created from the face of the earth. Yes, and I will destroy every living thing – all the people, the large animals, the small animals that scurry along the ground, and even the birds of the sky. I am sorry I ever made them."

He was sorry he had ever made people and decided to wipe us off the face of the earth. It says we broke his heart. So can things occur that are contrary to God's design, and he is not omnipotent? Can he in fact be surprised?

God decided to wipe out all life on this planet, not just mankind but plants, animals, and birds as well. I'm guessing not all the fish died. I thought God's issue was with his people and the way we were living. I know our actions have consequences beyond ourselves; is this why everything else was destroyed? I have started to feel like I shouldn't read Scripture anymore, because when I do I get more confused about God.

- Up through Abraham, Isaac, and Jacob, the Bible's focus on the relationship with God was that God would "give" to his people and they would "get" an inheritance, or have a legacy of kids with the family name, or acquire territory or land. This seems so human-centric. God said, "If you follow my commands, I will bless your family and be with you." This doesn't emphasize God as our Creator, but rather what he can or does provide.

In Genesis 17:1–8, God appeared to Abram and established a covenant with him:

When Abram was ninety-nine years old, the Lord appeared to him and said, "I am El-Shaddai – 'God Almighty.' Serve me faithfully and live a blameless life. I will make a covenant with you, by which I will guarantee to give you countless descendants."

At this, Abram fell face down on the ground. Then God said to him, "This is my covenant with you: I will make you the father of a multitude of nations! What's more, I am changing your name. It will no longer be Abram. Instead, you will be called Abraham, for you will be the father of many nations. I will make you extremely fruitful. Your descendants will become many nations, and kings will be among them!

"I will confirm my covenant with you and your descendants after you, from generation to generation. This is the everlasting covenant: I will always be your God and the God of your descendants after you. And I will give the entire land of Canaan, where you now live as a foreigner,

to you and your descendants. It will be their possession forever, and I will be their God."

It's all about one man, Abraham, and his ability to have descendants. I believe we're all God's children. Why did God make a covenant with only him? Scripture says he will bless the world through Abraham and the Hebrews. The Hebrews didn't even keep the covenant consistently, so why the blessing and the follow-through on the part of God? Was that just God's mercy for us: "I will give to you even though you don't deserve it," or did he not really mean what he said when he told the Hebrews the bad things that would happen to them if they didn't obey and follow him?

Is life about God blessing us with what we want? Is that what God is conveying through Scripture? Maybe, but in my heart it still seems like the core message of Scripture should be about God, not us and our blessing.

In the Old Testament, especially Genesis, I haven't noticed statements about a Messiah, love, or even much about an afterlife – hell or heaven. Abraham and his family were focused almost exclusively on their family, descendants, land, possessions, and blessings.

- How can God want to know something, as was stated in Genesis 18: "He had heard a great outcry because their sin is so flagrant"; then it says, "He's going to go down to see their actions." That seems an unnecessary step when he is all-knowing. This seems inconsistent and challenges my beliefs about both God and the Bible. Who is God if that is true? Or was this all a setup by God to make a point? Who knew what he was thinking? I can accept that he was known to have told things to Abraham, but I wonder what form God took during these interactions. I can't see how they occurred.

- In Genesis 18:22–33, Abraham challenged God regarding treating the righteous and the wicked the same:

> *The other men turned and headed toward Sodom, but the Lord remained with Abraham. Abraham approached him and said, "Will you sweep away both the righteous and the wicked? Suppose you find fifty righteous people living there in the city – will you still sweep it away and not spare it for their sakes? Surely you wouldn't do such a thing, destroying the righteous along with the wicked. Why, you would be treating the righteous and the wicked exactly the same! Surely you wouldn't do that! Should not the Judge of all the earth do what is right?"*
>
> *And the Lord replied, "If I find fifty righteous people in Sodom, I will spare the entire city for their sake."*
>
> *Then Abraham spoke again. "Since I have begun, let me speak further to my Lord, even though I am but dust and ashes. Suppose there are only forty-five righteous people rather than fifty? Will you destroy the whole city for lack of five?"*
>
> *And the Lord said, "I will not destroy it if I find forty-five righteous people there."*

Then Abraham pressed his request further. "Suppose there are only forty?"

And the Lord replied, "I will not destroy it for the sake of the forty."

"Please don't be angry, my Lord," Abraham pleaded. "Let me speak – suppose only thirty righteous people are found?"

And the Lord replied, "I will not destroy it if I find thirty."

Then Abraham said, "Since I have dared to speak to the Lord, let me continue – suppose there are only twenty?"

And the Lord replied, "Then I will not destroy it for the sake of the twenty."

Finally, Abraham said, "Lord, please don't be angry with me if I speak one more time. Suppose only ten are found there?"

And the Lord replied, "Then I will not destroy it for the sake of the ten."

When the Lord had finished his conversation with Abraham, he went on his way, and Abraham returned to his tent.

In his argument Abraham called it "only right" for God to destroy only the guilty, not the innocent. God seems to allow cause-and-effect results over and over and over. Both the guilty and innocent are often harmed due to the actions of the guilty. It seems the entire earth paid the penalty for the wickedness of people from the time of God's judgment through the flood. Here, God changed his stance based on an argument with a man. Why would he do that?

- Who captured so much accurate detail that it could be documented with credibility and confidence 500 years later? And how was this accomplished?

As I've already mentioned, as a writer with pens, pencils, paper, notebooks, computers, and more at my disposal, I know that if I don't write about an event within the first 12 or so hours after it occurs, I won't remember all the details and my account won't be an accurate reflection of everything that unfolded. When I don't write in my journal about something until the next morning, or even later that day rather than within a few hours, the details are nowhere near as clear and sharp.

The way of life in biblical times was of course different from ours today, but I still wonder how those writers preserved that level of detail about emotions and people's intent for hundreds or thousands of years. Did they have some type of system in 1400 BC and prior that enabled them to preserve those details accurately for thousands of years? Surely some documents were reproduced on other surfaces when the original became frail. But it still seems implausible considering the vast number of years involved.

- How did the distinct features of people stem from just one man and woman? Today there are various racial types; did that change begin with Adam and Eve, or did it occur after the flood? Or both? Our physical appearances are quite different, though these days the changes make us more of a mixture of characteristics rather than making us more distinct from one another. Did God originally create more people than just Adam and Eve? Were there more original races, spread in different parts of the world? My confusion persists.

  One potential or partial explanation could be that differentiation strengthens certain dominant human characteristics when groups become isolated and travel less over an extended period. It still seems incredible that we are as different as we are when our ancestry comes from one man and one woman.

- At Babel, groups of people scattered and apparently lost the ability to understand the common languages they had previously understood. What happened at Babel? How did God confuse them with different languages? Did God remove prior memory and knowledge? This is the first time that the repercussions of loss of knowledge really hit me.

- In Genesis 11:6, it sounds like God was surprised again, fearing that mankind would be united by one goal, speak the same language, and be able to do anything, even the impossible. From Genesis 11:4–8:

  Then they said, "Come, let's build a great city for ourselves with a tower that reaches into the sky. This will make us famous and keep us from being scattered all over the world."

But the Lord came down to look at the city and the tower the people were building. "Look!" he said. "The people are united, and they all speak the same language. After this, nothing they set out to do will be impossible for them! Come, let's go down and confuse the people with different languages. Then they won't be able to understand each other."

In that way, the Lord scattered them all over the world, and they stopped building the city.

By providing multiple languages God intended to confuse and divide us and cause us to not understand each other. That has sure worked throughout history, as division and misunderstanding have been the causes of many wars. It sounds like God wasn't aware that this would happen. What was being taught in these passages?

One interpretation could be that while God had told Noah and his family to "fill" the earth, and they were supposed to be spreading out, they instead stuck together and built one big city. The purpose of the multiple languages was to disperse groups of people so they would do what God had originally commanded. But I'm surprised that scattering didn't occur on its own as the population radically increased over time and in consideration of our disposition toward exploration and discovery. I don't think we'll ever know the exact reason why God dispersed the people in this way, but we are now spread across the earth.

- What does it mean in Genesis 6:9 where it says Noah was the only righteous and blameless man living on earth? Was he perfect?:

    This is the account of Noah and his family. Noah was a righteous man, the only blameless person living on earth at the time, and he walked in close fellowship with God.

    God had not yet provided Jesus's death on a cross as a sacrifice to pay for Noah's sin, which could have made him righteous or blameless in God's sight, so how could he be righteous? The Scripture reflects that all people have a sinful nature.

    If the writers of Scripture intended to convey that Noah was more righteous than many others, or was generally walking with God or seeking after God, why didn't they use that terminology? This is Scripture, so it's supposed to be perfect and directly from God. Was this just an error in translation at some point or did Noah not really exist and this is just a parable? I was raised to believe that Scripture is accurate and true unless it states that it is a parable. Based on so many other Scriptures and Noah's genealogy from Adam, that is documented with a family tree, it seems he was clearly a real person who had these experiences. I want to truly understand what was written and intended.

- After designing and creating everything in the universe, God intentionally destroyed everything 2,000 years later, except for what entered the ark as defined in Genesis 6:11–13:

Now God saw that the earth had become corrupt and was filled with violence. God observed all this corruption in the world, for everyone on earth was corrupt. So God said to Noah, "I have decided to destroy all living creatures, for they have filled the earth with violence. Yes, I will wipe them all out along with the earth!"

As an all-knowing God, he knew this was coming, so it seems this had to be an intentional part of his original plan, otherwise he would have designed it differently.

The Bible doesn't state how many people were alive at the time of the flood, but estimates by biblical scholars, according to the Answers in Genesis organization, range from 750 million to four billion people. That is a lot of people, the higher number being over half the number that populates our earth today! Even the lower estimate is twice the population of the United States in 2021. That's a lot of people to intentionally put to death, not to mention the billions of animals, plants, and insects that also died.

I don't understand what the creatures did to be destroyed. Were they just collateral damage? I can read the motive – because they were wicked – in the biblical passage, but I don't understand it in my heart.

- What happened to the Garden of Eden, and the two powerful trees – the tree of life, with the guardian swords, and the tree of the knowledge of good and evil? From Genesis 2:9:

    The Lord God made all sorts of trees grow up from the ground – trees that were beautiful and that produced delicious fruit. In the middle of the garden he placed the tree of life and the tree of the knowledge of good and evil.

Were they destroyed somehow prior to the flood, or also at the flood? Surely these were not normal trees, but unique, with life-giving powers. I would think a tree of life would live forever, unable to be destroyed. I'm surprised that in Scripture they are just referred to once, never again. Wouldn't trees that powerful have more history and a storyline, especially the tree with the flaming sword guards? That seems odd.

- According to Genesis 7:11, Noah was 600 years old when the flood came:

  When Noah was 600 years old, on the seventeenth day of the second month, all the underground waters erupted from the earth, and the rain fell in mighty torrents from the sky.

  In Genesis 6:3 God stated that a person's normal lifespan would now, or in the future, be no more than 120 years. Was Noah the last of the people to live hundreds of years? No. The Bible states that following the flood at least several humans lived a lot longer than 120 years. These include Heber, Salah, Reu, Serug, Terah, and Arphaxad. Even hundreds of years later, Abraham lived 175 years, Isaac 180, and Jacob 147. A generation after that, around 1700 BC (600 years later), people began to live for only 120 years or less.

My intent in researching the Bible was to rebuild my confidence in Scripture, not make it weaker and weaker. I know each of these questions can be researched much more deeply, potentially taking years for a single question, but because of my current capacity and how overwhelming it is to me right now, I haven't yet dug deeper on these questions. In my research I often found potential reasons for something being stated, but very seldom was able to land confidently on an interpretation that provided me with a satisfying answer.

When I sit in my recliner and read Scripture using the Bible app on my phone, the number of questions I have overwhelms me. For my own well-being, I want to stop. There is so much I don't understand! How can I continue to read and add more questions to my already mounting pile? They are weighing me down and suffocating my spiritual beliefs. I get mentally and emotionally exhausted, and I wonder how long I can continue to plug away at this!

I've gained great wisdom and value from the Bible, but my questions continue regarding its content and truth. I know my mind is limited, and that I can see things only through the mind I've been given and the teachings I've been exposed to. There is a lot of Scripture I don't understand. It's an unbelievably powerful book, no matter how we look at it, yet how we interpret it is critical to how it impacts our lives.

Chapter 13

Questions – God's Design

Is God one, or three, or even more beings? Who is Jesus? What does it mean to be "saved"? I have some pretty firm beliefs about the Trinity, and a lot of questions.

I'm reminded of the Chris Rice song titled "Smell the Color Nine." In it he shares how difficult it can be to fully know God. He uses the analogy of smelling the color nine: "Nine is not a color and, even if it was, you couldn't smell a color." That's how some of my questions feel. Maybe none of them have answers.

In this chapter you will get a sense of whether or not your questions are the same as mine.

I have already discussed some of the topics in this chapter from other perspectives. When a question or confusion surfaces in multiple ways and from various places, I know it will take a deep thought process to uncover a comprehensive answer, so please forgive some of my redundancy for the sake of revealing further mysteries.

God the Father

I typically think of God as being what the Bible called "God, the Father." I'm fully convinced of his existence. I believe he designed, created, and sustains everything that exists, so I don't question the perception of him as our Father.

Jesus

I'm torn about who Jesus is, and this is the hardest part of this book for me to write. My dad wrote and published a book about Jesus a few years ago because he thinks many people's beliefs about him are incorrect. He doesn't believe Jesus is God. He believes Jesus is the Son of God, but not God. There are numerous views and interpretations regarding Jesus's role in Christianity.

At my core, I believe Jesus came to earth, died for my sin, and was raised again to be with God. I decided to follow God and ask for forgiveness of sin at age nine. I have lived with the peace I've received from his forgiveness and from my access to and relationship with God. I think I still believe that when I die I will be united with Jesus – and God, my Creator and Father – yet it takes a more conscious choice of faith than it once did.

I'm not sure if my belief comes from the years of Christian teaching I received or from my current understanding. Wondering about Jesus's life prior to his three ministry years, during which he revealed his beliefs and teachings, has limited my focus on his ministry during my side-road journey.

More Questions

- In addition to the questions I raised earlier in my discussion about the book of John in chapter 4, I also want to know why God waited so long to send Jesus to earth. Using an approximate biblical timeline, Jesus was born about two-thirds of the way into earth's history.

- In Luke 2:52, how was this possible?:

Jesus grew in wisdom and in stature and in favor with God and all the people.

If Jesus is God, how could Jesus grow in wisdom and in favor with God – himself?

- According to Philippians 2:6–8, Jesus gave up his divine privileges:

Though he was God, he did not think of equality with God as something to cling to. Instead, he gave up his divine privileges; he took the humble position of a slave and was born as a human being. When he appeared in human form, he humbled himself in obedience to God and died a criminal's death on a cross.

Does this mean that as a human Jesus started with no wisdom, favor, or powers? If so, what part of him was still God? It appears that at a later point in his life he did again have at least some of God's knowledge, wisdom, favor, and powers. Did all of that surface at age 30, or did he grow into it over time and start to use it at the age of 30?

- John 3:16 states that God sacrificed his Son for us:

For this is how God loved the world: He gave his one and only Son, so that everyone who believes in him will not perish but have eternal life.

In what ways is Jesus God's son? Jesus wasn't birthed from the Father, since Jesus also existed in the beginning, prior to all things. My perception from Scripture is that in heaven he didn't grow up learning from the Father, and that he wasn't disciplined in heaven as he grew up. My belief has been that he didn't grow up – he didn't develop or go through a childhood in his eternal existence. I have not been able to find any of this addressed in Scripture other than the statement in John 1:1 that he, the Word, was in the beginning. This is different from our experience of a son.

Is it that he has the same essence, is perfect and holy, and made all the right choices to remain perfect while he was on earth? He had choice and could have made wrong or sinful decisions. He was tempted as we are. He left his heavenly home to go on a mission to redeem earth. He was dependent on the Father. Maybe these observations show how he was a son to God.

Or maybe he's the Son of God only in relation to his time on earth, though during that time he had more son-like experiences with Mary and Joseph.

- According to Matthew 15:24, speaking to a pleading gentile (not Jewish) woman in the region of Tyre and Sidon, Jesus said, "I was sent only to help God's lost sheep – the people of Israel." I wonder why Jesus said this, and if he meant it. While he was on earth it seems his message and service were for only the Jewish people. This is an interesting contrast to what God promised to Abraham in the Old Testament: that he would bless all the nations through Abraham.

- In John 10:16 Jesus said:

> *I have other sheep, too, that are not in this sheepfold. I must bring them also. They will listen to my voice, and there will be one flock with one shepherd.*

No additional clarification was provided in this analogy. We don't know who those "not in this sheepfold" were. Was he referring to others on this planet, or from beyond this planet?

- I wonder why God decided to send Jesus instead of just forgiving us and pardoning us as would a merciful judge (who doesn't make a person pay for their violation). He's God, not constrained. He could have designed this in whatever way he wished.

- According to Christian doctrine, the Holy Spirit is supernatural and is the third person of the Trinity. He provides direction for us to live God-honoring lives. Galatians 5:16–25 seems to say that only those "who belong to Christ Jesus," which I interpret as those who have been forgiven of sin and are born of God, are free of their sinful nature, direction, or guidance:

  > *So I say, let the Holy Spirit guide your lives. Then you won't be doing what your sinful nature craves. The sinful nature wants to do evil, which is just the opposite of what the Spirit wants. And the Spirit gives us desires that are the opposite of what the sinful nature desires. These two forces are constantly fighting each other, so you are not free to carry out your good intentions. But when you are directed by the Spirit, you are not under obligation to the law of Moses. When you follow the desires of your sinful nature, the results are very clear: sexual immorality, impurity, lustful pleasures, idolatry, sorcery, hostility,*

> *quarreling, jealousy, outbursts of anger, selfish ambition, dissension, division, envy, drunkenness, wild parties, and other sins like these. Let me tell you again, as I have before, that anyone living that sort of life will not inherit the Kingdom of God. But the Holy Spirit produces that kind of fruit in our lives: love, joy, peace, patience, kindness, goodness, faithfulness, gentleness, and self-control. There is no law against these things! Those who belong to Christ Jesus have nailed the passions and desires of their sinful nature to his cross and crucified them there. Since we are living by the Spirit, let us follow the Spirit's leading in every part of our lives.*

- When has the Holy Spirit been active on earth? Wasn't he available to us during our first 4,000-plus years? Based on John 16:7, he was sent only after Jesus was gone from the earth:

  > *But in fact, it's best for you that I go away, because if I don't, the Advocate won't come. If I do go away, then I will send him to you.*

  My understanding is that the Advocate mentioned here is the Holy Spirit.

- In John 14:15–17, Jesus spoke of those who loved him and obeyed his commands. Then he said he would ask the Father to give them an Advocate who would never leave them:

  > *If you love me, obey my commandments. And I will ask the Father, and he will give you another Advocate, who will never leave you. He is the Holy Spirit, who leads into*

all truth. The world cannot receive him, because it isn't looking for him and doesn't recognize him. But you know him, because he lives with you now and later will be in you.

Was the Holy Spirit limited in that he couldn't be here when Jesus was on this planet? According to the Old Testament, the Spirit of God or the Holy Spirit was active on earth before this.

- My understanding is that our conscience is a natural and normal part of all of us, built into us by God. Our conscience is not a person but rather a set of standards established in our minds, somewhat by nature and somewhat through learning. Our conscience reveals the difference between good and bad, and helps us deal with things that have both good and bad attributes or consequences.

- Both the Holy Spirit and our conscience speak to Christians in evaluating moral choices, if and when we take the time to listen, and sometimes even when we don't. Christians try to follow both their conscience and the Holy Spirit. When and how would the two be different; and when they are, how do we know if we're following the Holy Spirit or our conscience? If we're following either of them we're living a God-honoring life, so does it matter?

I believe in the Holy Spirit and I'm convinced I've had his leadership in my life, but now I'm not sure when I've heard my conscience rather than the Holy Spirit. Based on Scripture, it's critical to be looking to the Holy Spirit for daily direction. Are there times when it would be critical to discern whether I'm hearing the Holy Spirit or my conscience? Perhaps life is simpler for non-Christians who simply listen to their conscience.

- What happens when a Christian prays for God to reveal himself to a non-Christian? Does the Holy Spirit impact or direct the lives of non-Christians? Do non-believers have access to or communication with the Holy Spirit?

  I thought we all were given the power of choice to pursue God or not to, so would he change a situation that is related to choice? Might he motivate believers to take some action in regard to a non-believer that is not in alignment with the non-believer's choice? Does he use dreams, speak to them through the Holy Spirit, or influence them in some other way?

  God gave each of us choice. What does the Holy Spirit have the liberty to do? My interpretation of what I was taught is that non-believers don't hear his voice because they're not yet forgiven of sin and aren't yet in God's "family"; that God created them – in that sense they're his family, but not in the biblical sense of having sought forgiveness of sin and a relationship with God; and that the Holy Spirit does not live inside those who don't yet believe that Jesus is the Son of God.

- Why would God create a world in which people make sinful choices that result in pain and death? He knew our world would become sinful both before and while he created it. He knew we would turn from him and then he would destroy us with the flood. He knew of all the catastrophes, accidents, crimes, and atrocities that were to come.

God knew he would allow Satan to fall from grace and be given the freedom to be active on earth. According to Scripture, Satan talks to us, tempts us, and sometimes even affects our circumstances. God knew Satan would change Job's physical body and allow for the deaths of others.

But does God know the future? Does he know all that is to come? Does he know every word I'm going to say before I say it, and every day of my life before I even start it? I'm still striving to believe, in faith, that he knew our whole story before it began.

- Why design a system, world, universe, and creation like ours? What is the purpose? Where is the love in God's design? Does it allow us choice and lead to very few people being reconciled to God through Jesus? Even though there have been great effort and sacrifice made to share God's plan for mankind, as defined in the Bible, a very small segment of the world population over the past thousands of years has actually been reconciled to God in this way – between 2 and 10 percent in my estimation. Was that his design from the beginning? Are all the rest damned to separation from him eternally? If he knew the end at the beginning of all things, surely it must have been intentional, and I have a hard time comprehending such an intention.

- During our 6,000 or more years on earth, why hasn't someone been able to address these questions clearly enough so we all understand the one real truth? If there is only one spiritual truth, why can't we all, or at least many or most of us, understand it the same way?

How realistic is it to think that we can know the truth of why our universe was created, by whom, why we are here, how we got here, and what we're supposed to do while we're here? Can we discover it without doubt, or is the truth based on what we each put our faith and hope in? Is there a way to know where we come from, who God is, and what he desires, if anything? My confidence in the answers is lower than it has ever been. My Christian beliefs are dependent on faith more than ever.

- Choice is an interesting and critical topic relative to our spiritual beliefs. I was raised to believe that God built into people the ability to make choices. From these choices come the results we experience. The question is, does he ever take choice away or override it? I don't believe he overrides it, or at least not very often. I believe we usually reap what we sow. God will not take choice away from us because he designed us this way intentionally and perfectly.

The good news is, according to Romans 8:28, we can't make a choice that God can't use, and he can use them all for our good:

And we know that God causes everything to work together for the good of those who love God and are called according to his purpose for them.

This being true, all our little decisions aren't really that big of a deal. God can use them for good. We shouldn't fret about them, yet our choices create our futures. Each choice leads to specific opportunities and limitations. New doors are opened and others are closed based on our decisions. They're critical from the perspective that they create our futures.

- In Matthew 6:13, Jesus said:

  And don't let us yield to temptation, but rescue us from the evil one.

  This passage seems to tell us that choice is not a factor when we're tempted by evil. Does God deliver us from evil or the evil one, or are we required to make choices that keep us away from evil? If we make bad choices that lead to temptation or evil, we're usually going to receive the results of those choices. Are there cases in which God protects us from evil regardless of our choices? There might be, but it seems that many of our experiences of evil are due to choices, either ours or others', currently or in the past.

  Some translations of the Bible use the term "the evil one" instead of "evil." Can "the evil one" override a person's choice? Can he change the weather and create storms? What can he do that doesn't relate to our choice?

- In 1 Corinthians, 10:13, Paul teaches:

  The temptations in your life are no different from what others experience. And God is faithful. He will not allow the temptation to be more than you can stand. When you are tempted, he will show you a way out so that you can endure.

  What does "not allow the temptation to be more than you can stand" mean? Does God change the temptation, or the level of it, or does he help us deny our internal cravings? How does this relate to the choice he gave to us to make decisions on our own and do what we want to do?

When you have eaten and are full, but still have a strong desire to make another trip to the buffet line, does God prevent you from taking and eating more? Does he ensure there are no more clean plates available when you get in line, or that the item you crave is no longer available, or that the line has been closed and time is up? In this simple example you can substitute for "too much food" anger, jealousy, inappropriate sex, use of illegal drugs, excessive alcohol consumption, lying, cheating, stealing, and countless other temptations in life. I don't understand how God controls the temptation that we so often choose to place directly in front of us.

- In the Old Testament God sends nations and armies to destroy other nations and armies, as in the 2 Chronicles 36:17 passage:

  So the Lord brought the king of Babylon against them. The Babylonians killed Judah's young men, even chasing after them into the Temple. They had no pity on the people, killing both young men and young women, the old and the infirm. God handed all of them over to Nebuchadnezzar.

  God's actions seem to violate the choice he gave us to think the way we want to and to desire in our hearts and minds what we would like to have, whether good or bad. It says he "brought the king...against them." How does that work relative to the king's choice and free will? Shouldn't the king be able to choose whether or not to attack and destroy other nations? Did God truly "bring" the King against Judah, or was this the natural result in response to the behaviors of Judah, or somehow both, or neither?

- Scripture also refers to God hardening the hearts of certain people, as in Exodus 14:17:

    And I will harden the hearts of the Egyptians, and they will charge in after the Israelites. My great glory will be displayed through Pharaoh and his troops, his chariots, and his charioteers.

    How does that work relative to the Egyptians' choice and free will? Does "harden" mean they could not change their minds after a point? Does it mean God overrides our choices? Or is Scripture inconsistent in its description of God? A more likely explanation is that my mind is just too small and limited to understand God's management of free will.

- Based on what is taught in Scripture, what is salvation? From Acts 16:31, in the King James version of the Bible that I grew up with:

    Believe on the Lord Jesus Christ and thou shalt be saved.

    From John 3:16:

    For God so loved the world that he gave his only begotten Son, that whosoever believeth in Him shall not perish, but have everlasting life.

What do these verses mean? All my life I've understood the simple prayer formula, "Believe and you shall receive" (be saved or have everlasting life), but what does *believe* really mean, and what shall we receive? Is believing just thinking or speaking the right words about God even if you are manipulated into saying them or if your heart isn't in it? Are the words "I believe in you, Jesus. You are God's Son. You died and rose again, and you paid the price for my sin to God the Father," or do you have to additionally pray for forgiveness or receive it in some way? Are you a believer if you pray this once, or does it need to be said or felt repeatedly to put you in a state of being saved or having everlasting life? Is it a prayer at all, or does it define a life of relationship with God, prayer or not? Salvation, as defined by Scripture, clearly requires a belief in Jesus – who he is, and what he said and did.

- How much of what Jesus is reported to have said do we have to believe in order to be saved? What if we believe he is the Son of God, but have questions and doubts and aren't sure about all he is recorded to have said and taught? What impact does that have on salvation?

If salvation is dependent on forgiveness – a cleansing of our sin so God no longer sees it – is that a onetime event or does it need to happen repeatedly for us to have salvation? What if we totally change our beliefs down the road? If we prayed one time, is that all that is needed to receive salvation?

What if salvation weren't based on belief but rather on what we do, as Jesus said in Matthew 7:21?:

Not everyone who calls out to me, "Lord! Lord!" will enter the Kingdom of Heaven. Only those who actually do the will of my Father in heaven will enter.

This would indicate that salvation is not a prayer or a relationship, but rather what you do relative to God's will. What if it depends on an ongoing love relationship with God? If that's the case, what does that look like? What is required?

- What do we mean when we say we have "received salvation"? Is salvation a new level of confidence in who God is? Is it forgiveness for our sin – for doing things that separate us from God? Is it communication with God and the Holy Spirit that we didn't previously have, and if so, how does this communication work? Is it a new peace as we live, a peace we haven't previously had? Is it a new, clean, and pure heart – a start-over in life? Is it a new and different life here on earth? Is it access to heaven when we die, rather than to hell? Is it all of these or only some of these? It seems like quite a bundle of benefits. Maybe salvation is a kind of multipurpose blessing, not specific or easy to understand.

Imagine a person who has never gone to church, read a Bible, prayed, or communicated with God, but met a volunteer at a soup kitchen who led them in a prayer to believe in Jesus – just one prayer. Have they received salvation and eternal life?

How about someone who has attended church for years and has been taught the Bible but has never said a prayer asking for forgiveness? They honor God with much of their life and even give money to the church and to the poor. Does that give them salvation?

How about a kid who was raised in a Christian home and was taught much of the Bible at a young age, but doesn't go to church as an adult? Does the salvation they prayed for as a youth still apply if they're living a pretty respectable life, even if they don't pray, read the Bible, or go to church? What if they're not living a respectable life, and instead making many poor decisions that cause them numerous problems? Does that matter? Will they still receive salvation?

How about someone who has never heard of Jesus? They've never been to church, only know Christian people remotely, haven't read the Bible, and don't pray to God. What if they love the beauty of nature and Creation and live a good life? Are they saved?

How about someone who loves God, reads Scripture regularly, worships God regularly, and is in awe of Creation and our Creator? They don't go to church and don't gather regularly with other Christians. Do they receive salvation or do they need to have prayed a specific prayer asking for salvation at some point in time? And if so, does anyone other than God need to know that they prayed or turned to him?

From a bird's-eye view, salvation is profound and simple. When I dig deeper, it's more difficult to understand. It's hard to know how others feel about it, and it's difficult to explain to others what it means to be saved.

- To be saved means so much: you love God; you are in a relationship with him; you renew your relationship with him every day; you are in awe of him; you continually seek to know him better;

you try to honor him from your love for him throughout your life; you believe Jesus came from God, died, rose again, and paid the penalty for sin; and you've asked God to forgive the sin which has separated you from a *personal* relationship with him.

Does this seem too stringent? Or not stringent enough? If this definition is the requirement, are any of us truly saved? Or is salvation much simpler – just a one-time prayer in the heart and/or mind, with no further worship, relationship/prayers, or actions required?

- I don't understand *separation from God* relative to his seeing all and holding everything together. On one hand I have been taught that I am separated from God because of his perfection and my sin, which he can't tolerate, yet I've also been taught that he sees all and nothing is hidden from him, so how can I be separated from him? I don't clearly understand the difference between what can be called a personal relationship with God and a non-personal relationship with God. Is all our gratitude, awe, worship, prayer, and appreciation of him and his Creation considered personal, or are these considered personal only if forgiveness through Jesus has been provided? For now I continue to live with this lack of clarity.

- Paul, in Galatians 1:4, calls our world evil:

    Jesus gave his life for our sins, just as God our Father planned, in order to rescue us from this evil world in which we live.

Again, it seems God intentionally created and designed our world, and called it good, while knowing that evil would be coming. I believe he designed it the way he wanted it to be.

Some translations use the phrase "present evil age." I can see that Paul might have interpreted it this way, referring to the evil that was being lived out at the time he wrote this.

I don't understand God's design, with evil as a part of it. One could say that there was the *potential* of evil in the design, but because God knew what was coming in advance, it seems evil was a part of the design. It seems awkward that he created a universe that would embrace evil while he is a good and loving Creator.

- What does the Ephesians 1 statement concerning God choosing us before he made the world mean? Ephesians 1:4–5:

    Even before he made the world, God loved us and chose us in Christ to be holy and without fault in his eyes. God decided in advance to adopt us into his own family by bringing us to himself through Jesus Christ. This is what he wanted to do, and it gave him great pleasure.

    Does our holy and just God pick and choose in advance who will relate to him and who will turn from him and be destined to eternal separation and hell? How does our choice fit with this? This has been debated by Christians for years, and it's another mystery I don't understand.

- In the Old Testament, why would God designate a group of people – the Hebrews, or Jewish people – as "his own"? I realize that these passages were written by Hebrews, but if the Bible is God's holy word, conveyed to us through people, then this would have to be from God and be accurate and true. Aren't we all his people, his Creation? We all must ask for forgiveness of sin to have a relationship with him, so why does he call only one group "his people"? If he loves his Creation, including all people, what does that convey in light of his *chosen* people? The Jews being God's chosen people is also reflected in the New Testament. As I seek to know God better – to know his character – I wonder if I know less about God the closer I get to him. My limited mind seems to comprehend much less of him than I thought I had.

To me these questions seem basic and logical. I've had some of them in the back of my mind for years. They have been like a hamster on a wheel, going round and round. The wheel has seemed to be a good 20 or 30 feet away and off to the side, only in my peripheral vision. Now that wheel has moved right in front of my face. I can't avoid it or focus on other things any longer. And some of these questions have arisen more recently. Lacking answers to these questions has weakened my confidence in my beliefs, and in some cases even altered my beliefs. I'm not confident that very many of them will be answered for me during my lifetime, but I now feel the need to process them as best I can.

Not all Christians are as black and white in our beliefs as you might think. We have questions, and many of us want to continually seek and get to know our God and Creator better.

Chapter 14

Questions – Prayer

Prayer, especially what I call "asking prayer," in which we ask God for something, is a particularly puzzling topic for me right now. Writing down my thoughts about prayer feels like rebellion, or betrayal, and it's hard to be honest about what I think and feel inside about this critical topic. At times I want to pack my things and run away to a cave in a massive mountain and hide. I fear how my family and friends might respond, and that they might be offended by my questioning, especially on the topic of prayer.

But this is where I am, with an open heart wanting to know God better. Maybe you have had some of these same thoughts and have been afraid to think them or say them. I keep trying to provide background so my questions won't seem irreverent, wordsmithing these topics to death to ensure I don't offend or discourage those I love, while being completely honest.

God is God and we aren't. He knows all and knows better. In the core of my being I feel like a piece of dust who shouldn't be asking God for anything because I have no context for God's overall design. I don't know what would be best or right in respect to the big picture.

Asking prayers seem like well-intentioned, positive, baseless wishes or hopes for us to get something we want for ourselves or someone else. Yet I love the thought that saying you'll pray for someone is code for saying "I'm concerned for you [or about you]."

When I hear someone say "I'm praying for you," I receive it as showing care and concern. But I don't understand how we can ask God to intervene when he already has everything under control.

And we certainly shouldn't demand or claim anything from our awesome Creator of the universe. We're nothing compared to him. God remembers everything, so asking for the same thing repeatedly shouldn't make any difference to him. We simply will or will not get what we ask for.

Telling God something in prayer is for our benefit only. He learns nothing new, as he's all-knowing. I just hope it brings me closer to him when I have conversations with him.

When someone says "Please be praying about that," "Be praying for them," or "Would you please lead us in prayer?" I don't know how to respond based on my current doubts about prayer. At the same time I don't want to discourage them from their beliefs, so it's hard to know how to respond.

And the timing of our prayers is only for us – God is not limited by timing.

The following "well wishes" prayers are heart-felt and loving, but it doesn't seem that God intervenes as a result of such prayers.

To Rest

Some people pray for good rest, either for themselves or others. I think we control how long we rest, where we rest, and how often we do it. What would God change about that, especially if we make poor choices?

To Be With

Some people pray for God to "be with" someone. My current belief is that God is omnipresent. He's everywhere, all the time. Without his presence we would cease to exist. So I no longer know what to "be with him" means, as he is with us all the time. I understand we can choose whether or not to focus on him – that seems to be our choice.

To Bless

Some people pray for God to bless someone. I've not understood this one for a long time. What is being asked? How can God know what we actually want him to do, especially when we don't even know but just want things to be better from our perspective?

To Give Wisdom

Some people pray for God to give wisdom. As I've already shared, God has given us the resources we need to gain wisdom. It boils down to how often and how hard we elect to pursue it. Wisdom seems to stem from experience when my mind is open to learn. Does God provide wisdom without the experience or insight of others if we ask him for wisdom in prayer? If so, how? Poof... you suddenly know what you didn't previously know, and can act with that wisdom? It doesn't seem to me that God works that way, at least not often.

Seeking wisdom from any and every source available is always a good practice. The book of Proverbs is filled with verses that challenge us to aggressively pursue wisdom, to look for it everywhere, and to trade anything and everything to get it. We should seek to gain as much wisdom as we can, but it appears to come primarily from learning through experiences – our own and those of others who tell us or write them down. Scripture is one of those great sources.

To Heal

Some pray for God to heal. Again, God's natural laws seem to rule, and it's in his design whether or not we are to be healed. Our health is most often the result of our thoughts and actions, or the actions of others. We usually have at least some choice in the matter. This appears to be God's design.

Asking God to heal can come from a loving heart; however, in the full context of life, how can we know whether or not healing is God's will, or even in our best or his interests? Some illnesses, maybe even most of them, are self-inflicted through inappropriate behavior such as smoking; excessive drinking or using drugs; eating poorly; not exercising; stressing about things; not getting enough rest; lying; anger; and so on. Should he change our consequences because we ask him to do so? If so, we're asking for exceptions to his design. We can also experience negative consequences from others' choices, such as injury or death from an accident caused by a drunk driver.

To Encourage

Some pray for God to encourage someone, but each of us has been given the freedom to choose what we think, which leads to encouragement or fear. I don't see God overriding his perfectly planned design in order to answer this kind of prayer.

To Provide

Some pray for God to provide. Daily we reap what we sow, and what those around us have sown, to both our benefit and our hindrance. We don't get to personally choose where we are born, when we are born, our sex, our skin color, or our family. These are generally the result of the choices of those who came before us. But we take actions beyond these basics. We have been granted the power to work toward obtaining most of what we need or want. I don't see God making someone else provide for the need of another.

To Keep Safe

Some pray for the safety of others. As above, our safety comes from our choices and actions and those of others. I don't see God taking that choice away, and what remains is God's design and up to him.

I've had questions about prayer for a long time, but now I find myself avoiding situations in which praying and asking for prayers are commonplace.

I strongly believe that prayer should be filled with thanksgiving, listening, worship, wonder, and awe. There is much more purpose and value in listening to God than in telling, asking, or just conversing with him.

What If...

What if... God designed and perfectly created our natural laws, they function all the time without exception, and we can depend on them? What if his primary charge to us is to honor him by learning these laws and then learning to live by them and within them? What if we honor him even by not expecting or requesting exceptions to his perfect design? What if he wants us to be dependent on him, his perfect ways, and the design he provided through his natural laws. They're awe-inspiring when I look at them in detail:

- When you let go of something, gravity always makes it fall to earth. Gravity allows us to walk on the earth even when we're upside down compared to those on the other side.
- Day follows night.
- A planted kernel of corn produces a stalk of corn – not a green bean, or a coat, or a soft drink. We reap what we sow, and often even more than we have sown, both to our benefit and detriment.
- We have a responsibility to care for our physical bodies or suffer the consequences:

- Some things can harm us, such as heat, certain chemicals, and sharp objects. We need to handle them with care or avoid them.
- Without rest and sleep, we lose energy and can damage our bodies.
- We need exercise to stay limber and strong.
- We must consistently develop new routines, habits, and skills if we want to create new thoughts and muscle memory.
- We gain weight if we consistently take in more calories than we burn.
- If we don't use our minds and our bodies, we can lose the capacity to do so.

I think these observations about relationships fall somewhere in God's natural laws as well:

- If you yell at someone, they'll feel attacked and either clam up or attack back.
- The best way to be heard is to first listen well to the other person.

My thoughts above about prayer versus God's natural laws might sound like deism – the belief that there is a supreme being or Creator who does *not* intervene in the universe – but I do believe God intervenes in the universe. He holds everything together and sustains everything we have. And he can, when he wishes, change anything, even if it's integral to his design or natural laws. So I don't think I have become a deist, but there are ways in which I've moved closer to that thinking.

When we ignore natural laws, we're dishonoring our Creator. We all sometimes think we aren't subject to these laws – at least I do. When we ask for something in prayer we're implying that we don't want God's design to prevail; we're asking for an exception. We ask him to override his perfectly designed laws. That seems less honoring of him than accepting the natural consequences and reaping what we sow.

I really appreciate it when grace is extended to me when I don't deserve it, but I think we should strive to honor God with our actions *in accordance with his natural laws* rather than asking for exceptions, especially when we could have eliminated the need for the exception simply by taking better actions.

Does God Respond to Prayer?

I don't feel that prayer is made more effective by asking repeatedly, crying, screaming, displaying strong emotion, having more people pray, praying longer, or through *sequential* praying (such as a 24-hour prayer plan). If I request something from a counselor or a physician over and over, and I'm not willing to quietly wait and listen for a response or instruction, it would be annoying to them. Once they know my request, my role is to wait for a response, whether it's instruction, a prescription, or information to help me decide my next steps. Isn't that how God would view praying for something over and over again?

If I ask, I should wait to hear a response. Scripture tells us to ask, and ask, and ask, but that feels inconsistent with my understanding of an all-knowing God. Much of church prayer activity feels to me like gimmicks to sooth our consciences, or trying talk God into something. It doesn't feel right. I have not seen many of these activities reflected in Scripture.

God designed everything intentionally, specifically, and perfectly. His laws are right. They work, all the time. We reap what we sow, or are impacted by what others have sown, and we experience the consequences of these actions, pretty much 100 percent of the time.

My good friend's aunt was dying when I started to write this chapter. My friend poured out her heart concerning her aunt and her desire for her aunt's healing or recovery. She shared how heavy her mother's heart was because of her sister's condition. I felt badly that I couldn't respond in the way in which I might have in the past. My new feelings about prayer are strongly influenced by David's writings about God in Psalm 139:16:

You saw me before I was born. Every day of my life was recorded in your book. Every moment was laid out before a single day had passed.

Only God knows the big picture and plan. How can I ask anything, not knowing his plan? To request healing for my friend's aunt might have been contrary to his plan for her, so how could I pray? I could only share my heartfelt empathy about the pain and hurt my friend and her family were experiencing. I think that was also the heart of God, but that was all I could offer, and it felt like not enough. When I had prayed for someone's healing in the past, it felt good to extend hope and encouragement, but in the end it was usually disappointing. Is offering encouragement and hope in the moment enough for a loved one who is going through a health problem? Is that what I was called to do? Praying feels sincere, but the request is usually not granted in the way I ask.

Reacting appropriately to people I know who are in pain is important to me, but how can I pray with confidence relative to asking anything? I'm only confident in worshiping, praising, being in awe and wonder, and being thankful.

When I've asked God for something that I don't know much about, my prayers feel weak, or even fake – like a general wish. I don't know the big picture so I can't apply context to my request. Even in the best scenarios I probably know less than 2 percent of the whole picture. When I make big generic requests (Bless..., Be with..., Protect..., Help the people in India..., etc.), how would I know if they received God's support or action? How would he know what to do based on my request?

Since I can't know the outcome of my request, what am I really asking God to do? I feel like I'm voicing a global wish or hope, but if that's contrary to God's will, is my request even beneficial? Will the impact of my prayer be contrary to what God wants?

If my prayer is not already defined in Scripture, I should probably be asking God what *he* wants. It might be best to ask God how he would want us to pray for something, as Jesus did. In John 5:19 it says Jesus only did what he saw God the Father doing:

So Jesus explained, "I tell you the truth, the Son can do nothing by himself. He does only what he sees the Father doing. Whatever the Father does, the Son also does."

Maybe I should pray – or do anything for that matter – when I've heard from God regarding it. Maybe I shouldn't ask in prayer until I hear specifically from him and have a strong conviction that the request is consistent with his will. But what difference can it make to ask what God wants and then request it so he can do what he wants to? From James 4:3:

And even when you ask, you don't get it because your motives are all wrong – you want only what will give you pleasure.

This can be the case. But there have also been many times when I've prayed to ask for something for a loved one and I felt that my motive was pure and loving, yet the person didn't receive what I asked of God. When I deeply care for someone who's going through a tremendously difficult time – regarding health or otherwise – and I pray for immediate relief for them, is that a wrong motive? Was I wrong to request relief for Carolyn when she was in severe pain? My prayers were pure and from deep love. I can only believe that God seldom overrides our human choices and earthly situations.

Some would say that experiencing no change in response to prayer is simply a no from God. If that is so, how long should I wait to know that the answer is no? Is it immediate, hours, days, weeks, months, or years? A clear no would be easy to understand, but I've never sensed a clear no in response to prayer. Receiving a no response is difficult to interpret.

If I ask someone for something, I usually get what is in human terms an immediate response. The answer is either yes or no, or at least an indication that I might receive it at a later time or should ask again later. Seldom do I get no response, as though I haven't even asked the question. In the infrequent cases when this does happen, I feel disregarded, disrespected, or belittled. When praying to God, am I to keep badgering him until I receive a clear message? That doesn't feel right. It's difficult to understand what no response from God is truly supposed to convey.

Does God Change His Design?

In my experience, God doesn't change how his laws work, and that seems to be by design. People sometimes say their prayers have been answered. Someone might pray for a parking spot and immediately find one, but I think that's a coincidence, and that they have simply seen the situation as they wanted to see it.

I don't remember seeing any tangible, specific results from what I've prayed. And I've prayed for a lot in my first 64 years, including getting a job; someone else getting something they wanted; healing from sickness or injury; that a relationship would improve for someone; that someone would get out of jail, get a positive response from someone in authority, perform well in a competition, or get a good result from a mental or physical test of some kind; and on and on.

There have been times when something close to what I had asked for eventually happened, but I'm not convinced those were the result of prayer. It might have come weeks, months, or years after my actual request. Today I see these as natural results that came from people's choices and the passing of time – not a miraculous change God performed based on my request.

The word *manipulation* comes to mind when I hear someone speak about God changing something or someone. I could also use *change*, *alter*, *modify*, or *influence*, but the word that comes to my mind is *manipulation*. When I ask God to change something, it feels like I'm asking him to change or manipulate his grand and perfect design for the universe. He has set in place consequences for everything that happens, and I'm asking him to disrupt his design so I don't have to reap the consequences of my or someone else's actions. The Bible says a lot about prayer and encourages us to ask God for things, but today I don't understand how prayer fits with everything else that God has perfectly designed and set up.

Many of our consequences come from poor choices in the past — ours or others' — across the earth — such as poverty, genetic issues, and war. In this context the word *manipulate* feels like the most appropriate description of what we're asking of God when we ask him to change something from the cause-and-effect way it was designed to work.

Some people seek to see or experience miracles from God. I often see these as requests for exceptions to his perfect design. When people experience the birth of a child firsthand, they call it a miracle, and in my mind it truly is the miracle of life. And I would expand the use of the word *miracle* to reflect all of life and Creation. The birth process, our growth and development, healing and recovery, joy and sadness — I call it all miraculous.

Does God Hear Everyone?

According to my understanding of the teaching I have received from Scripture, we have access to our holy God only if we're forgiven of our sin. Some of this teaching probably stems from a passage in Isaiah 59:1–2, in which Isaiah is speaking to the people of Israel:

> *Listen! The Lord's arm is not too weak to save you, nor is his ear too deaf to hear you call. It's your sins that have cut you off from God. Because of your sins, he has turned away and will not listen anymore.*

But I currently believe God sees all — everything each one of us thinks, feels, and does. Does he turn a deaf ear to those whose sin is a barrier to him?

If someone is separated from God as a non-Christian, due to their unforgiven sin, then a prayer offered to God by that person is not received or accepted by God. Surely God *hears* and sees everything of mankind, but does he choose not to *listen* to non-Christians? Are life-threatening situational prayers and promises made by non-Christians of no value? Does it seem right that God wouldn't respond to them? I'm trying to understand if that can be true in consideration of God's spiritual design as defined by Scripture.

Based on what I've read in Scripture, a non-believer has access to God for just one thing: forgiveness of sin. I don't think God accepts their praise of him or his Creation, or a request for help, until they're forgiven of sin. Until the "sin gap" is closed, there is no access to communicate with him. Is that right?

Should I Pray?

What do prayer and having a relationship with God mean if God, the initiating and creating party, already knows every interaction, thought, and action we have? Where is the drama, interest, suspense, excitement, disappointment, and even reason for any of what we do if he already knows about it before it ever happens? This confuses me about how to communicate with God.

These days I'm hesitant to spend time sharing anything with God, who already knows me better than I know myself, unless I just need to put it into words for myself. He doesn't need it.

I've had questions about prayer for a long time, but now I find myself avoiding situations in which praying and asking for prayers are commonplace.

I strongly believe that prayer should be filled with thanksgiving, listening, worship, wonder, and awe. There is much more purpose and value in listening to God than in telling, asking, or just conversing with him.

Having a heart of concern and love is something I admire and hope I display often. It's God-honoring to feel another's hurts, celebrations, cries, longings, and other emotions.

These days when I pray, I don't ask. It hasn't seemed to change anything when I've asked in the past, so why should it now? When I pray I worship, sit in awe, and give thanks to God for who he is and all he has done.

So my interaction with God now is primarily sitting in the comfort that he is there, holds all things together, maintains our existence, and provides all that we need to live, enjoy, and endure the short time we have on earth. It's almost exclusively spending quiet time in his presence, being in awe of him and his Creation, and giving thanks to him for all that he is and has done for me and us.

This chapter was very hard to think through and eventually write, but it's an honest and open reflection of where I am. This is such a shift from what I've said and prayed in the past. These changes have come to a guy who has turned gray, and who knows, loves, and is in awe of our Creator/God.

Chapter 15

Questions – Church, Hope, and Religions

Beyond my questions about God, I have some regarding other spiritual topics, including how I should live out hope, and how my beliefs differ from those of other religions. My thoughts in this chapter aren't about mainstream Christianity; I'm continuing to drive down the side road, parallel to but not on the highway.

Church Services

From a young age, going to church has been a consistent and important element of my life. Now it seems to me that much of the service is conducted from a "man using God" perspective, with God loving us and helping us make it through everyday life. The focus seems to be on "God bless America" or "God bless me, my family and friends, my church, and my community."

I'm currently in an "America bless God" or "Let's all bless God" frame of mind. Focusing on us isn't the way I want to spiritually approach life. I want my gathering time with other believers to be all about God. Man was created and exists – just like the plants, animals, clouds, mountains, stars, other planets, galaxies, and the rest of Creation. I don't see these things as support or window-dressing for mankind, but equal parts of his intentional Creation, valued and enjoyed by him. It no longer seems appropriate to me to sing about and focus on us. I desire a "God above all" spiritual orientation.

The church services I've attended lately seem like personal-development training sessions in which we're taught to change the way we think or do some action. The motive is to please God. The actions we're urged to take are to be accomplished with his help, but they seem to focus on us and how we live. Sometimes the teachings are about how we interact with others, doing something to help others, changing our attitudes, or living with more peace and joy. But I work on my self-development on my own outside of church. I want my time spent in church to be focused on God and bringing more worship to him, and I think this difference can be demonstrated through the words that are spoken, the songs that are sung, and the activities that are shared. I seem to have a new and different framework for interpreting most of what I take in.

John Buckles, a friend and pastor, mentioned that I might be interested in reading a book called *Cat and Dog Theology* by Bob Sjogren and Gerald Robinson. He thought it reflected some of the same perspective. I read the book and he was right. I align very well with much of the content, and I highly recommend it if you're interested in a different focus than that at your church services.

"Me Management"

My "me management" on Sundays – to include an hour-long church service – has been exhausting due to both my recuperation from TBI and my revised spiritual beliefs. I stopped attending church, and my Sundays became emotionally and physically manageable. I no longer dread Sundays, anticipating days in advance the frustration of investing time to prepare for and attend a church service that doesn't speak to my need for worship.

Trigger Words and Phrases

There are some words and phrases I have difficulty tolerating these days. I have even walked out of rooms at church, and sometimes even the building, to get away from hearing them. Terms that once resonated with me now offend me and make me feel tense.

Sometimes they're in the lyrics of a song that's piped through the sound system into the hallways and other parts of the building. They don't ring true, and feel counter to everything I'm currently thinking and feeling. I would go outside for a while and then step back into the building to see if the song was over and if the next song was more consistent with my beliefs and focus. Sometimes I can even hear the song outside the building; if you're familiar with a song, hearing the music faintly or even just the beat of the drums or the bass guitar can be enough for the words come to mind. When this happened I would have to walk even farther away from the building. Situations like this are part of the reason I'm not currently attending church. Even some lyrics that are straight from Scripture create discord for me.

I have a hard time listening to words that reflect what I see as the "me, mankind, us" orientation, addressing our needs and God helping us get through or get by: "You are enough for me," "You are more than enough for me," "You will provide for *my* every need," and so on. These statements are very me-centric. I can't fathom that orientation when I face our almighty Creator. How can I possibly be concerned with whether or not God is enough for me? It feels off base relative to the whole of God.

Maybe there's a time and place to talk about what God has provided and is doing to or for us – the Psalms are filled with this. But right now, for me, with my current perception of God, I strongly desire pure worship of him for who he is.

"You will never let me down." Again, the focus is on us, or mankind. I can't even be in the presence of that perspective. It feels sick and off base. Life is not about me! And the God I worship and serve is too awesome for me to even begin to think this way. Pastor and author Rick Warren got it right in the first line of the first chapter of his book *The Purpose Driven Life*. He states, "It's not about you."

How can I be in a position to "accept" Jesus, or God, the Creator of the universe? I can't comprehend the concept. I think that perspective misunderstands our powerful and Almighty God. I think the intent is to "receive" the forgiveness and indwelling of Jesus. Maybe it's just a matter of semantics, but the word *accept* doesn't sit well with me.

When we address God, it seems like our only possible response should be awe, falling to our knees or on our face, raising our hands in worship, or sitting or standing in silence before our mighty Creator. I've tried not to judge, but in my current weak, limited state, I don't see other responses as honoring God.

My mom and I sat in her swivel chairs near the fireplace in her kitchen having a stimulating conversation. This is where she usually spends her morning quiet time with God and the Bible. We were talking about our spiritual journeys, and something she said triggered a word-picture that immediately got my attention. A big grin came across my face, and a new "Aha" came to mind. The image was looking through binoculars. Binoculars limit our peripheral vision while magnifying what's in front of us. In my word-picture, binoculars are targeted on a mirror straight ahead. It reveals that we're looking at... "us" in extreme detail.

I don't want to be narrowly focused on us or even just me. When I am, I feel like I'm missing the big picture of Creation and our Creator. In contrast, I want to be on the side of a large hill or mountain, with no hat, eyes wide open to the beauty of the sky, land, and sea. I want to stand there in awe and wonder, as Chris Rice's song "Wonder" states. Maybe I'm even spinning as I look up and see the sun and the clouds, or the moon and the stars at night. It's totally fine to become dizzy as I try to grasp and take in, from my one little perspective, a tiny piece of this Creation, in awe!

Hope

When I've prayed in the past for someone or about a situation, I hoped God would change the likely results. I don't currently cling to that type of hope because it's dependent on God changing his design for how things work. I've reprocessed what hope means relative to prayer and God intervening for us. I still want to live with tremendous hope, but it now means and looks different for me. My heart and mind have moved from asking to being confident that everything is in his plan, and to an even greater focus on what I can control.

I have the hope and confidence that we can intentionally change and grow. Our thinking drives our actions and feelings. We can see and work toward creating a better future, focusing on our potential and options and not on our limitations. I need to focus on what is in my control and be a great steward!

I encourage others, share my love and heart with them, join with them in their weighty experiences, hurt with them, and help them feel remembered. I want them to know that they matter. This is within my power. I want to be a bearer of hope and convey hope to others, even before they have it themselves.

World Religions

For the first time in my life I've been reading about other religions and beliefs. I used to be so focused on what I believed, in my own little world, that I never thought or cared about them in the past. I thought those of other religions had views similar to mine, with just a different outlook on how to achieve salvation or a relationship with God.

I learned that both Buddhism and Hinduism are focused on finding happiness in the here and now on planet earth. They're not about a supreme god, but more like a philosophy and a way of navigating daily living with an open mind and heart. Confucianism is about society and how we live. Judaism seems to focus primarily on serving our Creator and making sacrifices for sins – a form of salvation. Christianity and Islam focus on salvation and God. We all have different beliefs and focus on different things.

I assumed there were as many who believe in other religions as there are Christians, and that we all try to convert others to our beliefs. I now realize there are many who don't associate with any of these religions, following less popular religions, believing there is no God, or believing a hybrid of other spiritual creeds. The statistics below come from a 2015 report from the PEW Research Center. There are approximately:

- 2.3 billion Christians (31 percent of people who follow established religions)
- 1.8 billion Moslems (Islam)
- 1.2 billion not affiliated with any major religion
- 1.1 billion Hindus
- 500 million Buddhists
- 10 million Jews

Christianity is clearly the most prominent belief, though the number includes those who aren't close followers of their religion but identify with it culturally. I had no idea there were so few Jewish people compared to the number of Christians.

I was also interested to learn when each of these primary religions was founded. Hinduism and Judaism were begun between 3,000 and 4,000 years ago. Buddhism and Confucianism originated about 2,500 years ago. Christianity began about 2,000 years ago with the resurrection of Jesus. And Islam began about 1,500 years ago.

People's beliefs concerning God, the nature of life, how life should be lived, and why we exist run across the board. Some religions of course worship one God, yet that one God is different among those religions. Some worship multiple gods. Others don't even include a belief in a god. Beliefs about the afterlife are also different. I find it difficult to understand why people arrive at such different results when they're all seeking truth. It seems like the process should be simpler and clearer – like there should be someone who has the authority to say which belief is the right one. It comes down to faith, as we each elect to believe what we have heard or learned from what we believe to be a true source.

I wonder how many of us believe what we believe based only on what we were taught in our homes as young children. No other religion was seriously presented to me as an option while I was growing up. Christianity made sense and was supported by all those who were close to me, so I made the choice to be a Christian. I'm sure many others also didn't intentionally select their beliefs, but the support system around them was so strong that it was a natural process to identify with the family religion.

It is understandable to want our children to adopt the beliefs we hold to be true. As loving parents, we pass along our beliefs and biases to our children, and we protect them from seeing or hearing what we believe to be false or harmful. This now strikes me as limiting our children's choice based on comparing additional options, which is quite a shift in my thinking.

I belong to a group of five friends of various beliefs who meet weekly to discuss the big questions of life, which we call our Deep Questions Family. During a recent group call we were asked, "What is the one thing you would most like to change about the world?" My first and most heartfelt answer was that God and our origin would be clearly understood by all people and perceived by all in the same way, such that our knowledge of God is undeniably clear and the same for all of us. I would like God to be as clear to us as the moon – clearly seen by all to exist, within reach yet beyond us and not fully comprehended by any of us. Not the greatest analogy, but it covers some of the key points of my desire. I wish this because the differences in our perceptions of God cause so much confusion, turmoil, frustration, and divisiveness.

I don't understand why God allows this situation in which less than a third of the people on earth believe in him as the Christian God I've come to know. And I think that number is significantly overstated; some call themselves Christians based on cultural association, but they don't truly follow Christ.

These are some topics that I haven't even covered because I haven't yet processed my thoughts about them: the "sin gap" that prevents those who haven't asked God for forgiveness from communicating with him; the leading of the Holy Spirit; angels; heaven; hell; Jesus's death and resurrection; Jesus's prophesied return to earth; fasting; and evangelism, among many others. I've been so occupied with my big-picture topics that I can't yet concentrate on any of these.

My awareness of faith has skyrocketed. My faith is no longer automatic, but I make a conscious choice to believe.

Now

Chapter 16

Wonder

Are you a "big picture" person or do you live in the details? Maybe you're both, or neither, or maybe it depends on the situation. Can you see how your orientation might impact your life?

For years I've had a strong desire to live my life in context and not focus just on the detail in front of me. I want to understand the big picture first and only then consider the details. And for years I've gone on personal retreats that I call "Refocus Times," investing time away by myself to think about the big picture of my life. In my book *How to Refocus Your Life* I share my refocusing experiences and practices, the reason for them, the structure I use, the benefits, and other elements. Will Rogers said, "If you find yourself in a hole, stop digging," and I strongly believe in taking time to stop, get away, and gain clarity about my life. As I've turned gray, I've had an even stronger desire for a bigger, broader, and more holistic perspective.

A Timeline

A couple of years ago I joined my parents for a visit to the life-sized replica of Noah's Ark, called Ark Encounter, located in Williamstown, Kentucky. I enjoyed seeing that immense boat. It was interesting to walk through the multileveled structure, looking up and down and in front of and behind me to take in the complexity that may have been built into that massive boat.

As we walked the wooden hallways, the displays demonstrated how the animals might have been caged and how Noah might have managed feeding and watering the animals and removing waste. The detail that went into planning it was something else. It stimulated my thoughts regarding how the flood happened and how Noah, his family, and the animals made it through the flooding of the entire earth. The Ark replica is impressive.

I was even more intrigued when I saw the 22-foot-long timeline on the wall of the Ark called the *Adams Synchronological Chart or Map of Universal History*. My eyes were glued! It was first produced in 1871, so the original portion covered the time of Adam through 1871; and a newer portion reflects further events through 1900, which is a little over a 6,000-year period. It includes critical details and dates recorded in the Bible, and puts historical events and people in a visual context that shows what happened with whom, in what order, and how far apart events occurred from others. It's also endorsed by the Creation Museum in Petersburg, Kentucky.

It's eye-opening to read through this massive document – and it doesn't even include the last 120 years. My little 64 years is only 1 percent of the time covered by the chart. This is humbling. When I think of how important things sometimes seem, I realize that they're nothing in the context of mankind's time on earth.

If you believe in evolution, the significance of humans is even less in your eyes because you believe the earth and living creatures have existed for millions of years. Any way you look at it, we're a tiny segment of earth's history, but we have learned and done so much in the time we've been here. This was my biggest take-away from my Ark Encounter visit.

Of course I had to buy a copy of this document, and I've invested hours studying and contemplating it. I love the way it's laid out, which has allowed me to gain helpful context. It includes significant historical events and the dates of many key inventions, and enables me to put biblical characters' lives in perspective in terms of history.

I thought it would be an interesting exercise to divide our 6,000-plus years into 1,000-year blocks of time. Adam was created in year zero; Noah was born about 1,000 years later; Abraham at about 2,000 years; Solomon at about 3,000 years; Jesus at about 4,000 years; the Middle Ages occurred about 5,000 years after Adam; and I was born near the 6,000-year mark. These blocks of time provide a thought-provoking frame of reference for history.

I store my copy of the timeline, which folds into a 13-by-25-inch folio, under the futon in our middle bedroom so I can quickly reach for it whenever a question of historical timing surfaces during my quiet time with God. I might wear out the folds one day considering how often I open it. I'm thankful for this reference tool, and you might want to consider purchasing or borrowing one to gain perspective on our time here on earth.

How do you get context in relation to how you fit into earth's timeline? Yes, we're important; *and* we also represent a tiny segment in the grand scheme of time.

And a really crazy thing about time is that it's all the same to God. Knowing all, he doesn't need to learn anything as our time is played out and experienced by us.

This Place Is Breathtaking

If the timeline of humans is not enough to overwhelm me, all I have to do is observe the earth and the sky right in front of me. Seeing the vastness of our universe with my naked eye, or even with my telescope, puts the earth in a more humbling context. It's estimated that our solar system is about 36 billion times larger than the earth. I can't begin to comprehend that scale – and our solar system is a tiny portion of the universe.

When I think of the word *scale*, I remember the train sets I used to play with when I was growing up. I can appreciate the dimensions of an HO-scale train car that stands a little over two inches high sitting on the ground, next to a real 12-to-15-foot-tall train car sitting on railroad tracks. It would be easy to kick or step on the HO car as I admired and walked up to and touched the massive real train car. The scale is 1:87, which is an enormous difference – but nothing in comparison to that of the earth to our solar system.

On April 7th, 2020, I was home for the 21st night in a row, keeping my social distance to limit the spread of the coronavirus. At that time the United States had documented over 350,000 cases and over 15,000 deaths from the virus. Though massive, that number continued to escalate for well over a year, reaching millions of cases and hundreds of thousands of deaths.

I was watching TV, trying to pass the time, when I received a message from my friend and fellow ninja Shea Stammen. She typed, "Have you seen the moon tonight? It looks amazing! I know you love a good shot of the moon." I quickly rose from my recliner and headed to the glass sliding door that opens onto our back patio.

I stepped to the far end of the patio, and the sky was... overcast. I was so disappointed. It was like hearing there's a present at the front door, and you rush to the porch to open it with great anticipation, only to learn it's not addressed to you.

I headed back inside to watch more TV. During the news I heard that tonight's moon was to be the brightest for the entire year – what is called a super moon, or a pink moon. And of course the weather forecaster said it probably wouldn't be visible due to cloudy skies.

I stepped outside a couple more times during the next 90 minutes. On my third attempt, to my great surprise, I saw a wide-open, clear, dark sky, with the gigantic white moon appearing in between our roof and the roof of the house next to us. I couldn't believe it. My heart was racing with excitement! I peered at the moon from the far edge of our patio and was glued to the detail on the surface as I squinted to minimize the brilliance of the brightly reflected sun.

I ran into the house to get my cell phone to take some photos. (I had not yet purchased my telescope.) I took several – okay... a lot – photos of the moon from various angles, some with objects in the foreground obstructing my view, including the neighbor's tree and the roofs of our two houses. I was drawn to step back even farther, so I ventured out to the middle of our backyard basketball court. I stood there and stared in awe for a few minutes. I took even more photos and then decided to take some selfies with the moon over my shoulder. In my excitement I shared some of those shots with friends on Messenger. Then I stood and stared, wanting to take in as much as I could. I lost myself in the wonder of the sky, and eventually sat down in the middle of the court and just stared in awe.

I was reminded that there really is a large object out there, so far away and yet so close in relation to the other planets and dots of light off in the distance, and it really is held in place in space by God's magnificent design. It's not a white, two-dimensional spot on a photo or drawing – it's a real place. And we are only a tiny speck in the grand scheme of things.

A long, slow, drawn out "W O W" stuck in my brain, followed by another long and slow "H O W?" I couldn't fathom how God created everything and holds everything together. I was swept away to an extremely peaceful and profound sense of awe – "Wow... and How?" I felt like I finally had context regarding our existence.

We live in an incredible universe. From the massiveness down to the minutest detail, it's overwhelming to observe and contemplate.

The Detail

During my quiet times I sometimes look around simply observing things. One day I was fascinated by the eye-level dust I saw on a bookshelf in front of me. It's hard to imagine being fascinated by dust, but I was. I'm responsible for dusting as one way to contribute to the operation of our home. The dust was not supposed to be there, at least not for much longer if I was doing my job properly.

I began to wonder how dust is generated. My initial thoughts led me to the general movement in our home, and the process of dirt being transferred from the outside to the inside. I was also reminded of the natural decay of everything. Everything starts new, and over time breaks down, decays, and falls apart. Much of the dust I saw was likely tiny particles of decay from the things in our home, including my skin. It's an amazingly complex process that occurs continuously. Everything is designed and has a process.

One day I sensed that God was giving me a theoretical assignment to see how I would respond. He was asking me to consider what it would take to design one blade of grass. My impression was that he wanted me to determine:

- How it would start
- How it would grow
- What it would need to grow
- What color or colors it would be
- How its color would change over time, and in what conditions
- How wide it would be
- How high it would grow
- How thick it would be
- How pointy and sharp its sides and tip should be
- How it would die

- How long it would take to die
- How it would generate new grass – or if it would
- What functions it performs for other parts of Creation
- How it would adapt – or if it would – to changing conditions such as folding, draught, heat, and cold

I could go on and on, but that one little suppositional assignment overwhelmed me with the complexity built into one blade of grass.

You can take that little assignment and expand it to include all types of grass, and plants, and trees, and animals, and then humans. It's overwhelming. Spending time contemplating our existence like this feels healthy and freeing to me. It leads me to feel more in awe of God and to have greater appreciation of who he is and what he's done and is doing. What an enlightening perspective! We have an awesome, unbelievable God!

Although I didn't come away with well-defined conclusions from this exercise, it provided me with a tremendous amount of peace and clarity. My breathing felt clean and deep, and I felt renewed. It gave me an enhanced sense of context about our physical world. My perspective is as a layman, not a researcher or a scientist. If I had more knowledge and context, I'm sure I would be significantly more impressed and in awe of the complexity and details of Creation.

Carolyn purchased two copies of a children's book called *Indescribable: 100 Devotions for Kids about God and Science* by Louie Giglio. One copy was for our grandchildren and one for me. It has been an enjoyable read each day as I learn more about God's impressive Creation. Take, for example, the 200 times per second a bee's wings must flutter in order for it to fly, or the creative expression in the design of a sea horse – a fish unlike most other fish. I enjoyed reading and fully appreciating how fish don't live in air like we do.

Reading it led me to ponder their unique and completely different design. It's truly *Indescribable*!

The Immensity

Some days I look out the window at a small portion of the stunning sky. It's immense! The clouds are so impressive; and then you have our sun, just one star in the sky.

It's difficult to comprehend the power contained within our one star. For it to cease for even five minutes would be disastrous. It's beyond comprehension to understand all that the sun provides for us. Without it we and all life on earth wouldn't exist. Most of us take it for granted most of the time, including me. It's just there and does what it does while we live our lives – taking showers, attending meetings, writing emails, keeping up on social media, cooking meals, doing dishes, and everything else.

The Size of the Universe

In 2019 I made a special trip to the Creation Museum in Petersburg, Kentucky. I was excited to see if I could learn anything that would provide me with additional perspective or insight for my spiritual journey. I moved through the entire museum at a quick pace, wanting to make sure I saw everything. I planned to go back later in the day and visit the areas that particularly caught my attention.

I was familiar with most of the content in the museum. I made my way through the lines of people in front of each display, slipping my way through large families and strollers as I moved through the "7 Cs of History" displays. These start with the Garden of Eden, continue with the Flood, and so on. (The actual Cs are *creation, corruption, catastrophe, confusion, Christ, cross,* and *confirmation*.) I've had a lot of Bible teaching, and the exhibit was consistent with concepts I knew and understood.

I looked forward to the two 20-minute-long planetarium presentations: "Created Cosmos" and "Aliens: Fact or Fiction?" I sat through both and was even more impressed and in awe of Creation and its size. "Created Cosmos" makes the point of how little the earth is relative to Creation. It includes a lot of extraordinary images of what I already appreciated – the massive size of our universe. It's something else! I left the presentation even more convinced that earth, the place we call home, is a tiny speck of dust in relation to Creation.

When it was over I wanted to stay in the dark, leaning back in my cushioned chair, and stare at the ceiling display with my mouth hung wide open in awe. All I could think was, "Wow... and... How?" I look into Creation and continually think, "Wow... God, how did you design and establish all this?"

The Number of Stars

Later, at home, sitting in my recliner in our middle bedroom, I looked up what astronomers believe to be the total number of stars, or suns. I wanted to know the number we can see with just the human eye, and the number visible using our most powerful telescopes.

The *Sky and Telescope* website states that with our naked eye, under the best conditions, we can see about 4,500 stars. That site also states that astronomers put current estimates of the total stellar population at roughly 70 billion trillion (7×10^{22}). I can't imagine 70 billion trillion anything, let alone stars. How can we possibly begin to comprehend that number?

When someone thinks something can't be done, sometimes they make the point by saying, "not even a one in a million chance," or "not in a million years," thinking there is absolutely no way that thing could be done. If someone said there was only a one in a trillion chance that God created other forms of life somewhere else in the universe, there would still be the potential for 70 billion other life forms to exist somewhere in our universe. I'm not sure what I believe about life on other planets, but when I think of the possibilities in those terms, it really blows my mind. This universe, that we know just a little about today, is so massive!

The Distance to the Moon

The moon is about 238,900 miles from the earth. That is equivalent to over 85 trips from Los Angeles to New York. If we could drive to the moon, at 70 miles an hour, the trip would take over 3,400 hours. That is 141 days of straight driving, 20 weeks with your foot on the gas pedal, or about five months of continuous cruise control.

I was curious how long it would take a bullet to get to the moon if it could maintain its speed all the way there. A bullet travels at about 1,700 miles an hour. It would take a bullet 140 hours to get to the moon, or nearly six days. It's so far away compared to distances we are familiar with on earth, and yet it's close to us relative to our closest star, the sun.

The Distance to the Sun

Our sun is 93 million miles away. That is millions, not thousands! Driving at 70 miles an hour it would take a little over 1.3 million hours to get there. Driving 24 hours a day, it would take 55,300 days – 151 years – of driving.

The bullet would take nearly 55,000 hours to reach the sun – 325 weeks, or over six years. The earth, the moon, and the sun are only small parts of our solar system. This is a big place!

The Distance between Stars

I was also curious about how far we estimate stars are from each other. One estimate is that they average over four light-years apart. A light-year is the distance light travels in one earth year. One light-year is about six trillion miles.

I purchased a Newtonian reflector telescope with a 130mm glass optic objective lens. With this I can see features on the moon and some of the features of other planets and objects in the night sky. It helps take me one little step closer to God's extraordinary design. I'm more impressed each time I take my telescope outside and view the details of the crater-filled surface of the moon, especially the craters on the very edge of the sunlight, where you can see deep shadows that give depth to an otherwise flat-looking vista. Unfortunately we have so many cloudy nights here in Columbus that I don't get to use it as much as I would like. I joked with Carolyn that the person who packed the telescope and shipped it to Ohio was probably laughing and saying to a co-worker, "This is the first time I've ever shipped a telescope to Ohio; with all the cloudy days they get, they will never get to use it." At times it seems that the imaginary conversation is right on.

An Out-of-This-World Experience

We all see impressive images in magazines and books, on TV, in the movies, and on the internet. It's moving to look at shots of the Grand Canyon, Arches National Park, the moon just above the ocean, or the Eiffel Tower. It's fun to look at and appreciate these special places.

We move to a radically new level of appreciation when we stand on the Eiffel Tower looking out over the city of Paris, or under the Delicate Arch in Utah, or on the edge of the Grand Canyon looking both across and down the canyon. When we see these things live, we also feel them, and they become a part of our life experience. In a way they change who we are.

One night I was admiring the detail of a nearly full moon from my front yard. It was so bright and sharp that night that I got out three different tripods, one each for my binoculars, my camera, and my telescope. Through a telescope the moon has detail and personality, and looks more like the real place that it is. I decided to see if I could find and focus on Jupiter. I pulled up the telescope application on my phone, and sure enough, it was visible that night, not far from my view of the moon. I swapped out my 10mm eyepiece for a more powerful 6mm lens, and added a 2x magnifier. Jupiter is about 1,600 times farther away than the moon. To the naked eye it looks like a very bright star, but like the moon it's only reflecting the light from the sun. I was able to aim my telescope at Jupiter and see it with my own eyes – not a photo, a rendering, or a computer-generated image – this really was Jupiter, with its moons. It was difficult to keep my telescope still enough, because the target is so small that any touch of your hand or eye makes the image jiggle. Within a minute or so I was able to see it clearly. Wow! It was so great to see it with my own eyes.

There was another fainter dot of light in the sky, above and to the left of the moon. The app showed that it was Saturn. My eyes lit up even brighter and I decided to see if I could see Saturn as well.

Due to the rotation of the earth and light pollution, it's difficult to spot the tiny lights in the sky through my telescope. They appear, then move quickly from right to left in the little eyepiece. I used my spotter scope to narrow my aim, adjusted my telescope, and after only a few moments I saw a bright little dot zip across my eyepiece. I backed it up and managed to center the light in my scope. It was blurry, so I adjusted the focus, and as the telescope became still I clearly saw Saturn! The rings were astonishing, and so distinct! That amazing image kept me awake most of the night, and it became a poignant part of my life experience. I had been granted a new glimpse of God's incredible Creation!

The next night as I was out enjoying the night sky, Carolyn came out to see how I was doing. She was able to see three moons orbiting Jupiter. That was so fun. Our solar system is amazing!

Cloudy Days

One Saturday morning in late January, I was sitting in our middle bedroom gazing out the window and listening to a worship song. It was cloudy, with cold rain. I didn't feel anywhere near the immensity of Creation and God as I do on a sunny day or a clear night. I thought how most of us love sunny days, which I do as well. I love the awesome impact of seeing and feeling the power of the sun shining down on me. And without cloud cover I feel the potential of seeing beyond the blue sky and out into space.

I've always appreciated getting to see a bigger perspective. When all I see is clouds, they can cause me to feel limited, closed in – even trapped in a small space – and I miss the context of the big picture. I work hard to appreciate cloudy days, knowing there's a big universe and a powerful sun on the other side. But it's sure nice when I get to see the sun and the blue sky and bask in their presence; and I also love to connect with the expanse of the night sky.

Cycles to Everything

I'm drawn to the cycles of life. Everything seems to have a cycle. I'm impressed by the cycles of the sun, the moon, and the earth, which give us days and nights and tides. I'm awed by the cycle of the seasons, and the differences in those cycles depending on where you are on earth. And of course there is the cycle of life for all living things – people, trees, squirrels, insects, flowers, and on and on. The differences in the life spans of turtles, flies, dogs, whales, snakes, etc. are amazing. Another wondrous cycle is the eating and processing of food, in which waste from an animal can become fertilizer for a plant, and then cycle back to another animal that eats the plant. From the healing process to life, death, and everything in between, it all has a cycle!

I could invest days, weeks, and much longer appreciating the mind-blowing processes of all these cycles of life. God has put so much into his design for Creation.

Interconnected and Interdependent

I've been stopped in my tracks when I've thought about the interconnectedness and interdependence of God's design: the cycle of oxygen for people and animals to breathe and the resultant carbon dioxide for plants to breathe; the bee's pollination from plant to plant; the impact of sun, soil, and water on plants; and the need for daytime and nighttime, to name a few. One animal eats another animal, keeping its population under control, thus keeping the population of its own species under control. Everything seems to have a purpose, and is connected. I'm in awe and wonder of every aspect of our existence and how it works.

I encourage you to take some time to sit and observe the impressive Creation around you, pondering both the immensity and the detail. Think about the cycles that exist, and notice the interdependencies. I'm convinced you will come away in awe. At the very least, we should not take God's Creation for granted. This is an astonishing place, created by an amazing God.

Chapter 17

What Resonates Now

We search for places, people, and activities that reinforce what we believe. I love to meditate about passages of Scripture and songs that reinforce what I feel in my heart.

I can strongly relate to certain portions of Scripture. It's comforting and encouraging to see ideas that are in my heart and my mind reflected in the Scriptures. It's extra validation, deep within my soul. I don't feel alone. Some authors of Scripture saw God the way I'm seeing him.

Below are a few passages from the Old Testament that closely resonate with my perspective on God and Creation.

Job 38

I can relate to Job being confronted by God, not because I've experienced the same thing but because I relate to some of the questions God asked Job – which remind me of the questions developing in me as I turn gray – as revealed in Job 38:3–10, 19–20, 24–27, 31–33, and 37–38:

> *Brace yourself like a man, because I have some questions for you, and you must answer them. Where were you when I laid the foundations of the earth? Tell me, if you know so much. Who determined its dimensions and stretched out the survey-*

ing line? What supports its foundations, and who laid its cornerstone as the morning stars sang together and all the angels shouted for joy? Who kept the sea inside its boundaries as it burst from the womb and as I clothed it with clouds and wrapped it in thick darkness? For I locked it behind barred gates, limiting its shores.

Where does light come from, and where does darkness go? Can you take each to its home? Do you know how to get there?

Where is the path to the source of light? Where is the home of the east wind? Who created a channel for the torrents of rain? Who laid out the path for the lightning? Who makes the rain fall on barren land, in a desert where no one lives? Who sends rain to satisfy the parched ground and make the tender grass spring up?

Can you direct the movement of the stars – binding the cluster of the Pleiades or loosening the cords of Orion? Can you direct the constellations through the seasons or guide the Bear with her cubs across the heavens? Do you know the laws of the universe? Can you use them to regulate the earth?

Who is wise enough to count all the clouds? Who can tilt the water jars of heaven when the parched ground is dry and the soil has hardened into clods?

God's questions would make anyone ponder their perception of Creation. They provide me with a sense of God's power.

I wonder how these words were heard by Job, and how they were documented to this level of detail and then passed down eventually to the author of the book of Job.

Moses, on Holy Ground

Whether I'm sitting in our anti-gravity chair under the tree in our front yard, stopping to sit on a bench in the shade during a walk through our nearby park, or driving down a quiet road facing the sunset, I'm regularly engulfed in a sense of the awesomeness of Creation and of God. Often my awareness of God is overwhelming. The emotion feels like what Moses must have felt at the time of the events in Exodus 3:1–6:

> *One day Moses was tending the flock of his father-in-law, Jethro, the priest of Midian. He led the flock far into the wilderness and came to Sinai, the mountain of God. There the angel of the Lord appeared to him in a blazing fire from the middle of a bush. Moses stared in amazement. Though the bush was engulfed in flames, it didn't burn up. "This is amazing," Moses said to himself. "Why isn't this bush burning up? I must go see it." When the Lord saw Moses coming to take a closer look, God called to him from the middle of the bush, "Moses! Moses!" "Here I am!" Moses replied. "Do not come any closer," the Lord warned. "Take off your sandals, for you are standing on holy ground. I am the God of your father – the God of Abraham, the God of Isaac, and the God of Jacob." When Moses heard this, he covered his face because he was afraid to look at God.*

I don't cover my face, but my experience of respect, admiration, and awe are like Moses's.

Psalms

For years Psalms has been my favorite Bible chapter. It reflects the awesomeness of God, and our limitations. It's packed with bold statements and insights concerning God and mankind.

In Psalms, David describes God and some of his attributes. All my life I've believed in this description of God. It boldly proclaims the information as the truth. As I explained earlier, I now wonder about the validity of these verses. This is one man's perception and description of the God he worshiped. How can we possibly know if it's true? I share these verses to provide the background for my beliefs — Psalms 139:1–18:

O Lord, you have examined my heart and know everything about me. You know when I sit down or stand up. You know my thoughts even when I'm far away. You see me when I travel and when I rest at home. You know everything I do. You know what I am going to say even before I say it, Lord. You go before me and follow me. You place your hand of blessing on my head. Such knowledge is too wonderful for me, too great for me to understand! I can never escape from your Spirit! I can never get away from your presence! If I go up to heaven, you are there; if I go down to the grave, you are there. If I ride the wings of the morning, if I dwell by the farthest oceans, even there your hand will guide me, and your strength will support me. I could ask the darkness to hide me and the light around me to become night — but even in darkness I cannot hide from you. To you the night shines as bright as day. Darkness and light are the same to you. You made all the delicate, inner parts of my body and knit me together in my mother's womb. Thank you for making me so wonderfully complex! Your workmanship is marvelous — how well I know it. You watched me as I was being formed in utter seclusion, as I was woven together in the dark of the womb. You saw me before I was born. Every day of my life was recorded in your book. Every moment was laid out before a single day had passed. How precious are your thoughts about me, O God. They cannot be numbered! I can't even count them; they outnumber the grains of sand! And when I wake up, you are still with me.

I look at these verses in a new way, with the hope that they're true, with faith that they're true, but with the fear that maybe they're not. Today it takes more faith for me to believe they're true. I feel like the father in the book of Mark, chapter 9, who said to Jesus when he wanted Jesus to help heal his son, "I do believe, but help me overcome my unbelief."

Songs of Worship

In chapter 3 I wrote about how important singing and playing guitar were to my faith years ago. My turning-gray thinking has me seeking out songs that worship God and his Creation rather than focusing on our needs. When I hear or sing worship songs, I feel God's presence and my connection to him, and they lift my heart.

"Wonder" by Chris Rice reminds me of the new awe I feel for God's Creation. "Indescribable" by Chris Tomlin shares how uncontainable God is, citing examples in the stars, the sea, and the seasons, which really click for me. "Adonai" by Petra (*Adonai* means "Lord" in Hebrew) uses ideas from Scripture and calls God an endless mystery. "How Great Thou Art" by Carl Boberg is an old hymn that cites the wonders of nature. These are the kinds of songs that lift my spirit and allow me to appreciate the words along with the beautiful music.

Look them up online and you can read all the lyrics, which I can't reproduce in their entirety here due to copyright laws.

As I mentioned, I hope to play my guitar more in the future and get the music back into my fingers as it was when I was in college. Some of those great old worship songs I used to play may yet have me swaying back and forth again with my guitar.

I'm encouraged when I read Scriptures reflecting where I am on my spiritual path. I'm thankful for the songs I've discovered that lead me to worship, reflecting the beliefs of the deepest parts of my heart. I'm so grateful for the wonder and awe.

Chapter 18

My Firm Beliefs

Some of my beliefs have remained quite firm. Having been on this recent spiritual journey for over three years, I still remain confident about five of my core spiritual beliefs:

1. God is outside of what we know as time and space.
2. God knows all, and has always known all, including the past, present, and future.
3. Everything was designed and created by God, and he sustains it. His work is intentional and not random.
4. God created and established natural laws, and they always hold true.
5. Part of God's natural laws is the power of choice given to mankind. Because of our ability to choose, we experience cause and effect. We also experience what other people have caused.

So much of my worldview stems from these statements. Below I explain each of these a little further.

God Is Outside of Time and Space

Because God is the Creator, he must have existed before anything. He must also exist beyond the end – of humanity, of our world, and of time – if there is an end. As Scripture states, he knows every word every person says before they say it, if I'm interpreting Psalm 139 correctly.

He must also be beyond what we know as space, which includes everything, including our atmosphere and outer space. My belief is that he existed before he created our time and space. This really is impossible to grasp. Even though I can't understand it, I still believe it based on what I've been taught.

God Knows All

It's difficult to comprehend what it means to know all. As babies we know nothing more than how to breathe, eat, cry, poop, and sleep. We grow and learn throughout our lives, accumulating wisdom and knowledge based on our experiences and learning from others. Our knowledge compounds as we build on each new thing we learn. So how can we begin to understand the concept of knowing all, including everything that ever was and ever will be – the design and workings of everything? Having the knowledge of each being and thing that has ever existed or ever will, including every animal, fish, plant, man, woman, planet, star, and galaxy, is beyond comprehension.

This belief declares that God is above all. There is nothing to compare to him. That's why descriptions of him never sound adequate. This includes referring to him as King, being above all other gods, and so on. To me these descriptions fall way short.

The belief that he's all-knowing has tremendous implications. It impacts praying to him to ask for something. I know so little, and he knows everything, so how can I possibly know what is truly good and right to ask for? I don't have the context to know; only he is in a position to know what should take place.

My belief that God is all-knowing stems from my extensive Bible teachings. I might or might not have come to this conclusion just by observing nature. A couple of key passages that have led me to this belief appear in Psalm 139, a passage I shared earlier. Verse 1 says, "You know everything about me." Verse 4 says, "You know what I am going to say even before I say it." Verse 5 says, "You go before me and follow me." And in verse 6, "This is all too great for me to understand." Verses 13 through 16 make several bold statements in this regard:

You made all the delicate, inner parts of my body and knit me together in my mother's womb. Thank you for making me so wonderfully complex! Your workmanship is marvelous – how well I know it. You watched me as I was being formed in utter seclusion, as I was woven together in the dark of the womb. You saw me before I was born. Every day of my life was recorded in your book. Every moment was laid out before a single day had passed.

This means that nothing has been, or ever will be, a surprise to God. And God knew that giving humans free will would result in positive and negative consequences for this planet and the people, animals, and plants on it. All these consequences are intentional, and by design. He would have designed things differently if he wanted different results. This is hard to swallow, but if he knows all, designed all, and created all, it must be intentional.

Everything Is God's Design

I continue to be in awe at the complexity and interdependence of how the universe works – gravity, quarks, cells, DNA, electromagnetism. It's so complex that I can't imagine it wasn't designed.

Carolyn and I have the greatest appreciation for the number and kinds of birds that visit our bird feeder – all the various sizes, colors, and behaviors. Think of the ability of the human body to see, hear, touch, smell, and taste, and the immense abilities to think, feel, fear, love, desire, and be disappointed. Our inner processes, such as food digestion, reproduction, and healing, demonstrate interdependence; when one breaks down, that impacts many other parts of our body.

God's creativity is exhibited in the massive number of types of animals, plants, and people. There are many varying estimates ranging much higher, but All You Need Is Biology stated that a total of 1.3 million species have been identified and described, and there are many more alive on Earth. The most accurate census, conducted by Hawaii University, estimates that 8.7 million species live on this planet. These include animals, insects, fish, and plants. There are over 390,000 documented plant species, including 60,000 species of trees. And 86 percent of terrestrial species and 91 percent of marine species are still to be described. God's creativity is mind-boggling.

How can people be so similar (two eyes, a nose, two arms, two feet, a heart, a brain, etc.) and yet be so different? All this natural complexity could not have occurred by chance – that's more mind-boggling than to believe it's by design. Both options take faith, and to me less faith is required to believe that it is the Creator's design.

God's Natural Laws

God's natural laws always work. We benefit from them and pay significant prices because of them. I've discussed the laws of cause and effect pretty thoroughly already.

The Origins of My Beliefs

I wanted to understand where each of my beliefs comes from, so I categorized them into three buckets:

- from my personal observations and non-biblical sources
- from biblical teachings
- supported by both of the above

Beliefs from Personal Observations and Non-Biblical Sources

Most of these beliefs are consistent with what I've understood from the Bible, though they're not spelled out in the Bible. They include things like we need air, water, food, movement, and rest; and everything decays – nothing gets better in the long haul and even wine goes bad at some point. The consistency has caused me to continue to place high confidence in the Bible.

Beliefs from Biblical Teachings

In addition to the beliefs I've discussed to this point, these include that God is love and we're called to love God and one another, God defines how we are to behave as sexual beings, and God provides laws to live by such as the Ten Commandments. The following teachings are also from the Bible, but it takes a lot more faith, rather than a simple understanding or belief, for me to know beyond a shadow of a doubt that they're true.

- Sin is "missing the mark" of God's requirement to live perfectly in everything we do, all the time. There is a gap between how we live and what God requires of us.
- God has a son, and his name is Jesus.
- Jesus lived a perfect life on earth, and then died to pay the price for our sins so that we can have a relationship with God and be forgiven.
- God called the Hebrews his people.

- The Bible defines how mankind will end and describes an afterlife.
- Heaven exists. It's a place to live eternally in the presence of God. There will also be a new heaven and a new earth that will replace our current Creation after the last judgment.
- Hell also exists. It's a place to live eternally in the absence of God.
- We're to share our beliefs with others, providing them the opportunity to decide whether or not to believe in a Christian God.

Beliefs Supported by Both My Personal Observation and Non-Biblical Sources, and Biblical Teachings

- We're totally dependent on God and Creation to survive on this planet. We need the sun, the earth's rotation, gravity, the cycle of air and heat and cold, etc.
- Time marches on at a consistent, steady pace. It's our most limited resource. We can't go back. Time passes no matter how we waste or invest it. Our time on earth as we know it will someday cease to exist for each of us.
- We have the freedom and ability to make choices, though some restrictions are imposed by our environment or by other people.
- From birth, by nature, humans are selfish. We think mostly about ourselves.
- We live by believing in much we don't see, which creates both our hopes and fears.
- We'll do almost anything to survive and preserve our bodies, families, and possessions.

- We must work to provide for ourselves, or someone else must do the work for us.
- Everything is based on cycles.
- We usually reap what we sow, and usually much more than we sow. We plant one kernel of corn and get a whole stalk with many kernels.

There is a good deal of consistency and congruity across these three categories that supports my past strong beliefs. If my personal observations were more inconsistent with what I've learned from the Bible, I'm sure I would have had much more conflict in my heart. I'm grateful that my observations strongly support what I've learned from the Bible, and I remain in deep peace, feeling that I'm on the right track with my beliefs.

I could consider other spiritual beliefs in my quest for answers about Christianity. I could learn more regarding Islam, Mormonism, the Jewish faith (although I have a basic understanding of the Jewish faith from the Old Testament), Hinduism, and other Eastern religions. But my questions aren't inspiring me to do so at this time. Maybe in the future I will learn more about these; time will tell.

I continue to be convinced that God is revealed in the Bible. Christianity has a strong hold on my heart. I feel God's love and peace deeply within, and I'm thankful for that. Christianity feels true based on what I've observed of mankind and our universe. Even amid my questions, I still have rocks of belief I hold to. They still strongly impact how I see the world and live my life.

Chapter 19

A Broader Perspective

I have a new and broader perspective on some things since embarking on my side-road journey after my concussion. This can be both energizing and quite disturbing, but I'm thankful that new insights, perspectives, and clarity have surfaced.

New Perspectives and Insights

One of the occupational therapy exercises I was taught during my post-concussion rehabilitation was to focus on an object and then jump my eyes to another object at a different distance and quickly focus on that. It's easy to do this by holding your finger several inches in front of your face and using it as one of the objects on which to focus. This exercise helped my eyes work in tandem.

It's harder than you might think to quickly focus on your finger upon moving your eyes from an object across the room or in the distance. One evening this hit me as an analogy of where I am in my spiritual journey. As I turn gray, and since my concussion, the things that are the sharpest are the big-picture elements of my life. I'm having a lot harder time seeing clearly and sharply the detail right in front of me. I see the awesomeness of our Creator and Creation, and the details of the earth and mankind haven't been as important.

A one-year-old sees a limited view of the world. Everything they understand is in relation to themselves and what they want. Everything they see is reality. It's true and it exists – the rattle, the bottle, the room in the background, Mommy and Daddy wearing clothes. All of that is right in front of the baby, yet it's not the full picture of their existence.

If we widen the view a little for this hypothetical child, there is a neighborhood outside of that home, with other people taking showers, cleaning their houses, playing games, sleeping, laughing, crying, and sometimes yelling at each other. There are cities where thousands of people are working, countries, continents, planets, solar systems, galaxies, and a universe, all functioning at the same time.

The baby's perspective is real, but it's extremely incomplete. Through time, growth, and maturity, it will experience a larger perspective that provides much more context for doing what he or she will eventually do.

My turning-gray spiritual experience has significantly moved me from a general focus on me, my family, my city, my state, my country, mankind, and sometimes our world, to a much greater appreciation of our solar system, the stars, the galaxy, and our universe. They dwarf our world – the earth we live on that seems insignificant relative to the whole of God's Creation. I'm still trying to better understand how to incorporate this larger picture in my day-to-day life and activities.

Stronger Feelings

Much of my current thinking isn't new to me, but rather I have a stronger awareness of the power and truth of my thoughts. I have stronger feelings about each of the topics I've discussed above, especially these:

- The wonder of the sky, moon, stars, mountains, ocean, sun, and nature
- Earth's timeline from a biblical perspective

- Our thinking impacts everything we do! Our thoughts lead to actions, which lead to results.
- Our choices, both goal-based and automatic ones, also lead to actions, which lead to experiences, which create our environment and memory, which lead to our future choices.
- Everything seems to compound!
- People who seek God see who he is and what he wants quite differently from one another. There are many religions and sources of spirituality, and none are fully accurate or easily and totally understood by all of us.

A Different Focus

When I'm with a group of people who outwardly appear to have the same thoughts and beliefs I have, I'm more aware that how they interpret and live those beliefs might be quite different from the way I do.

To say I'm a Christian puts me in a category even though some of my beliefs are different from those of other Christians. I live in a particular environment, so how I worship, pray, counsel, and support others can be quite different from what other Christians do in other environments. I'm designed by God to be a specific way, and my assumptions, actions, and choices are different from those of others.

Some Christians focus on preaching about hell so that others will choose the path of salvation. Others are caught up by the love of God. Some concentrate on the awe of Creation. Others use their time to fight sin in our world, some concentrating on what they believe to be vital issues such as human trafficking, abortion, and homosexuality. There are those who want to be in church anytime the door is open, maybe for the love of being with other Christians or due to feeling guilty about what will happen if they're not always there. Others have no desire for church, but can't wait to be in nature, admiring God and his Creation. Some of us have elements of several of these viewpoints, but usually one or two in particular are strong in our hearts and minds. I believe that stems from how we see God as individuals. We might have similar core beliefs, but we walk them out differently based on what we have experienced and lived.

Rather than be frustrated by this, I choose to celebrate these different worlds we live in, which were designed by God before we were born. Our different worlds aren't a surprise to him. We should be happy and content with our individual world, whatever it might be, and focus on knowing God better and maximizing our stewardship and potential while we're here. I choose to be thankful for my world and to do my best to honor God the best I know how.

Perspective Makes All the Difference

What we see leads to what we think, feel, and do. We *look* at the same things, but we don't *see* the same things. We see things differently based on the environment around us.

During our 40th anniversary trip to Banff, in Alberta, Canada, I was reminded of the power of perspective. In taking photos of the beautiful mountains and landscape, the perspective of the camera made all the difference in what was seen by those who looked at the photos. In some cases I took wide-angle shots to take in an entire mountain range. In other situations I zoomed in to snap a specific mountain. Sometimes I focused on a distant mountain and left the foreground not quite in focus, and in others I did the opposite. Sometimes Carolyn and I were in the foreground with mountains or other scenery in the background.

Camera angle is critical to what I want those who will view the photo to see. I can shoot from straight on, from the side, or looking upward, as I did when we rode a chairlift to the top of a mountain, or downward, as I did when we were on mountaintops. I might wait for a cloud to be positioned in the shot, or for one to pass out of range. How I frame a shot makes a difference in what I and others see in the photo.

How we frame our beliefs is much the same. We can see our beliefs, or parts of them, from many different angles and perspectives, which all color our thoughts and actions.

I hope I'm widening my view or perspective of God and Creation, but I know I can go much wider and still not see the full picture. I've seen some good close shots of Creation, and I don't want to lose any of the perspective I've had in the past, but I want to continually build on it as I live life and seek the truth about this impressive place and our awesome Creator.

Endurance versus Deliverance

Several years ago, while walking on my treadmill, I was thinking about two impressive ideas: endurance and deliverance. I'm not sure why these words appeared on my heart, and I couldn't identify any current situation that specifically related to either of them. I searched my life experiences to see if I could find a match, but I couldn't.

For years I let the two concepts marinate in the back of my mind. Over time I began to see them as themes for how to honor God in living my life. It seemed the message I was to learn was to value endurance more than deliverance.

The more I thought about it, the more I believed that enduring a situation, rather than being delivered from it, leads to conforming more closely to the image of Christ. "Becoming like Jesus" is a strong theme in the Scriptures. The charge is to take him into your life and let him live through you.

When we're delivered from an experience or a choice we've made, we don't have an opportunity to grow. Most growth, spiritual and otherwise, comes from enduring situations and challenges. I believe this is a healthy, long-term, spiritual approach to life, and I do my best to approach challenges with this in mind.

Awe

I've never felt this much awe. Taking time to slow down, stop, and allow my eyes to study and my mind to wonder about Creation is awe-inspiring. As I've mentioned, I can do this just sitting in my recliner looking out the window. I can also do it on our basketball court with my binoculars or telescope pointed to the moon, or when I'm walking through or sitting in a park, or, thankfully, in many other situations. I used to be critical of people who said, "I will spend my time with God in nature." Now I'm one of them. ☺

There is so much to observe! It's real, and it's right in front of me, all the time. When I stop to really *see*, I feel close to God and experience a much stronger sense of the reality in which I live. Quiet observation is now at the top of my list of ways to be in awe of God, and I would rather spend my time in awe than in any other way. It also feels like excellent stewardship in which I'm honoring God. Spending time with him in this way just feels right.

Worship

These days I feel drawn to worship God, our Creator, and admire his Creation, which seems to go on forever. I'm drawn to spend time with him, conscious of him and immersed in his Creation, taking it in with my eyes, ears, nose, body, and even taste buds. These senses are phenomenal. I want to experience them to the fullest and to be immersed in the sensations God provided as I soak in his Creation. These days I don't ask of him as often. I would rather worship him.

Thanks

I'm fully invested in being thankful and appreciative to God in the depths of my soul for what I have. Being an excellent steward includes continual thanks for all he has provided. I've been granted an unbelievable life. It's my duty to be thankful and not take it for granted. I want to be a person of ever-increasing thanksgiving.

God's Pleasure

It seems likely to me that God took great pleasure in creating our universe with its tremendous complexities and interdependencies, and that he also takes pleasure in observing mankind and what we do, animals, plants, oceans, clouds, winds, seasons, birth and death, and the cycles of everything.

He must take tremendous pleasure in what he created beyond our speck of a planet. No one on earth knows if God created other forms of life – intelligent or not – on other planets, but I'm convinced he created the universe for a reason even if it seems beyond the needs of life on earth.

Since my concussion, some things seem much clearer, including my awareness of Creation, how our minds work, how we see things differently from one another, how natural laws dictate how we live our lives, and how awe, worship, and thanks are due to our Creator, who enjoys his Creation.

Chapter 20

Pursuing the Big Picture

I'm writing this on Easter. It's a major day of celebration, and yet it's not. For the second year in a row, Easter is a difficult day for me. I celebrate the resurrection of Jesus along with my entire Christian family around the world… kind of. I'm trying to celebrate with my mind, but my heart's not in it. I'm hesitant in my thoughts and actions when the songs are sung, the words are spoken, and the empty tomb is celebrated.

I feel like I'm on stage, in a choir, when the glorious final song is being belted out with the loudest and clearest heartfelt notes being sung by each member of the choir… except for one – me. I feel like I'm there with my eyes open wide, I'm moving my lips with the words being proclaimed by the others, but there is no voice with my words, no sound coming out, and no emotion on my face. It feels much more… hollow. I feel like I'm singing alone even though there are others standing by my side. I'm wondering why I'm remaining on the stage with this vibrant group of people. In faith, I believe the message of the powerful songs, but not with emotion. Even my faith is hesitant and with questions. Though I'm singing, I don't feel like a member of the choir.

I'm still dealing with several major questions and conflicts in my mind relative to who God and Jesus are, and they impact how I celebrate Easter. Because I'm not confident about who Jesus is, I can't appropriately process his death and resurrection. I believe Jesus came to earth, died, and that God raised him from the dead, but who was God raising?

I want to simply believe – to be back where I was in the past – but I can no longer get there. It reminds me of when I learned the truth about Santa and the Tooth Fairy. Once I realized they were make-believe, it was impossible to go back to fully believing in them.

It's also like I'm in a small cage with bars on all four sides. There are two other connected cages, one to my right and one to my left. The one to my right contains the Christian beliefs I have had all my life. The one to my left contains beliefs such as atheism, agnosticism, and paganism. I'm locked in my cage and can't get back into the cage to my right or travel back and forth between the cages.

I've not fully landed on what to think about some of my prior beliefs, but that doesn't seem as critical as my new focus on honoring God's Creation. I don't seem to even want to spend time thinking about my prior beliefs when my current awe of God seems so much more important and holistic. I have clearly experienced a major paradigm shift in my thinking.

I want to go back to where I was before spiritually, but my new perspective of God has changed everything. I can't fully comprehend that Jesus is God; that there is a separation between a non-Christian and God; and that Jesus, as God, came to earth. These beliefs sound true, and I want to believe them, but I can't fully reconcile them with the questions in my mind. I can only believe them through faith, which is the only way anyone has ever been able to get there. They aren't automatic parts of my faith as they once were. I can now only get there as a mental choice – consciously choosing to believe these doctrines even when they don't seem right.

The Three Facets of My Life

What are the major components of life? Are they body, soul, and spirit; or heart, mind, and soul; or something else? My current frustration is like living with a fractured bone that no longer aligns with the rest of my skeleton. Or like a gear system in which the cogs are no longer aligned; they don't fit and move together, at least not well. Or like I'm listening to three people who have great voices, singing together in three-part harmony, which can sound so sweet, except they're singing in different keys. Individually they sound beautiful, but together they sound terrible. I would love to listen to them one at a time, but it sounds so terrible that I have to get away. The three voices are individually strong, like what I think of as the three major facets of my life – the Creator and his Creation, Christianity, and my day-to-day life; the goal is to get them to align in my heart and mind.

Christianity and my day-to-day life have always fit well together. The greatest spiritual tension I faced was meeting people I cared about who were not Christians, but that is to be expected. The Bible teaches that not everyone follows Jesus, and maybe not even many.

The two "gears" in which I now operate are my awe of God and the details of my day-to-day living. The "gear" of Christianity doesn't get much use. That might change if I discover a renewed priority for earth and mankind relative to the other elements of God's Creation. I can't seem to be in awe of God and do much of anything else. I feel like I must leave my awe state to address day-to-day life, and then I can jump back into awe mode. Christianity is hard to focus on. It doesn't fit well with either my focus on God's Creation or my day-to-day life, though it seems it should.

Ways I've Pursued a Big-Picture Perspective

Having a big-picture perspective has always been important to me, and now it's more important than ever. For well over 20 years I've taken the time to go on personal retreats, as I mentioned above.

Sometimes I'm at a Panera, either facing a window so I can observe nature and the activity outside, or, in the cold of the winter, in front of the gas fireplace. Sometimes I'm sitting 10 or 20 feet from a beautiful lake with a blank pad of paper, a pen, and my "Refocus Time" outline. Wearing my wide-brimmed, olive-green hat, and sunglasses, I stare out at the landscape and the wildlife. Being in and enjoying the mystery of Creation feels peaceful and comforting. The details of my day-to-day life fade away in light of the beautiful, slow, consistent cycles of life.

Sometimes I drive a few hours away and sit on a bench in a small town square looking for a new and fresh perspective on life. Being in new and different places helps pull me out of my thinking rut and consider the big picture.

I've journaled daily for years, which oddly can provide context for big-picture thinking. In contrast to what I'm saying to myself about my day, I write about what I objectively *should* be saying to myself about my day. One is emotional and the other is much more rational. Among other topics, I document lessons I've learned from the day's experiences and things from that day that I'm thankful for. It feels good to capture each day by reliving some of it, learning from it, and being thankful for it. Another valuable and precious day has then officially passed. I come away with appreciation for the day and better focus and motivation for the days ahead.

I also spend time assessing my experiences. I've conducted a self-assessment for every coaching session I've ever provided to a client. I try to do that immediately following a session, whether it was in person or over the phone. I want to evaluate how I did and how I can make the next session even more valuable for my client.

I've done the same with speeches I've given and meetings I've led. I evaluated every meeting I conducted during the two years I was the president of the local International Coach Federation chapter. Before going home I would head to a nearby fast-food restaurant, purchase a drink, and then sit, unwind, and replay each segment of the experience in my mind, identifying what went well and what didn't. While things were fresh in my mind, I identified things I could do differently to make the next meeting even better.

As John Maxwell said, "A lesson is repeated until it is learned." I want to learn from each experience so I don't have to repeat any negative ones. I want to be an excellent and wise steward of the life I've been given, and these assessments help me step away from the detail of the execution to evaluate the experience from a broader perspective. I value the big picture and I believe I'm a better person today because of all these assessments.

Chapter 21

My Life Now

Having shared a good deal about my journey, in this chapter I hope to convey where I am spiritually and non-spiritually, at least as I finish writing *Turning Gray*. It's been a long three-plus years of searching and learning. My views have become somewhat clearer through this writing process, just as I had hoped. Maybe your thoughts about your faith are clearer as well – or perhaps muddier than ever. But questioning ourselves can lead to new beneficial thinking and transformation.

How Am I?

When I'm in a controlled environment, without loud sounds, multiple sounds, and bright lights, I feel most like my pre-concussion self. Because I usually control my environment, and wear ear plugs and sunglasses when I need to, I have much of my previous capability most of the time. Sometimes I have to retreat to a quiet place. There are still situations that set me back for a few hours, or even days in some cases. What makes it extra hard is I don't always know what will provoke a relapse. My focus is a little different, but I'm living much like I did prior to my concussion.

From a spiritual perspective, I'm living with a much broader view of God, with less focus on praying for things and more on observing Creation. Mostly due to the sensory overload, and partially due to the focus of the services on mankind, I'm not currently going to church. I'm happier with the sound of a natural breeze through the trees. "Breeze through the trees" actually describes my worship time ideal quite well. I let God provide my music naturally through his Creation. And I prefer natural sunlight to artificial lighting. I simply want to be with God in his Creation.

I love to spend time in the mountains – my "mountain time." As small as they are relative to the surface of the earth, and especially in comparison to the universe, they provide helpful context for how little and insignificant I am in relation to Creation. I love to stand at the base or on top of a mountain and look out at the broad, engulfing, panoramic view, slowly from my far left to my far right. It makes me feel so small and insignificant, and yet at peace. If I didn't love taking photos so much, I would just stand or sit there and observe the immensity, detail, and beauty for hours.

Carolyn and I have taken some wonderful trips to see and admire beautiful mountains. We've been to Hurricane Ridge in the Olympic Mountains of Washington; Cottonwood Pass, Breckenridge, Pike's Peak, and Aspen in Colorado; Mount Hood in Oregon; the Zailiyskiy Alatau mountains in Kazakhstan; Mount Pilatus in Switzerland; and many others. Remembering each of these mountain ranges brings a tremendous smile to my face and joy to my heart.

Since my concussion we've made two incredible trips. In October of 2018 we visited Ouray, Telluride, Silverton, and other towns in the San Juan Mountains of Colorado; and in September of 2019, as I mentioned above, we went to the Canadian Rockies. These two trips were just what I needed when I was recovering, having spent so much time inside, often in the same recliner. I needed to get out and see the world, and it was therapeutic to feel like a part of this incredible Creation!

Give me mountain time, enjoying God's Creation, and I'm a happy camper, with a lot of life context. If I lived in the mountains I might feel differently, but I'm ready for a lot more of them now. In the back of my mind I often hear the kids' song that goes, "I love the mountains, I love the rolling hills, I love the flowers, I love the daffodils...." God, thank you for the mountains.

My Top Priorities

I'm pleased when I can engage in activities that incorporate my priorities:

- Enjoying life
- Enjoying and building relationships
- Having meaningful experiences
- Learning and growth
- Contributing to others, my community, and beyond

Enjoying Life

I've prioritized enjoying life because I want to honor God in all he has provided. I believe I bless him when I enjoy the life, resources, and experiences he provides. I enjoy taking a shower; a good night's sleep; my breakfast; my quiet time with God each morning; my thinking and planning time; writing books; sharing life with Carolyn; reading; looking at the moon through my telescope; playing at the ninja gym; spending time with my family; sharing my thoughts with my Deep Questions Family; and so much more. I reflect my enjoyment through creativity, smiling, laughing, tasting various foods, learning, discovering new things, growing... there are many ways to enjoy experiences and express that joy.

I believe enjoyment is a choice, and that my attitude is within my control. We can elect to enjoy almost anything if we want to. Sadly I don't always make that choice. You might not either, but we can. We just need to see things as part of God's divine plan and find the blessings in them, even if we don't see them clearly in the short term. During my recovery over the past few years it's been hard to make that choice at times, but I know it's the right perspective. I try to think this way as much as I can.

Relationships

Relationships are a priority because without them life is quite lonely. Everything is better when it's shared with others, especially those you love. We were designed to be relational beings, but it's easy to get too busy to invest time in our relationships, which can result in an empty, lonely heart. I try to ensure that I'm continually investing in my relationships. It can be taking a current relationship deeper, sharing an experience with someone instead of experiencing it by myself, or meeting new people.

Each week I call my parents in Wichita to maintain my long-distance relationship with them, and I try to make the 16-hour trip to Wichita at least two to three times a year. Carolyn and I talk or meet with Tim and his family in Cleveland at least monthly, and are in weekly contact with Michelle. I check in with members of my ninja family on a weekly basis to see how they're doing, and over the years I've met with friends over lunch or breakfast on a regular basis. Having accountability partners has been a powerful way to deepen relationships. All these relationships are very important to me.

Experiences

New experiences can create a new appreciation for life. It's easy and comfortable to stay safe at home and not experience much of the outside world, but it cuts us off from so much. New experiences contribute to new perspectives and potentially to new relationships. The same is true for doing something we've done often in a different way. Going on a trip to somewhere we've never been allows us to see new things, feel new feelings, and relate the new to what we've already experienced, expanding our understanding of the world.

Some of my family's special experiences are tied to sports. We've attended Michelle's *American Ninja Warrior* competitions and have been to other ninja competitions at new gyms and in various cities, getting to meet new people. We've gone to OSU basketball and football games, seeing and meeting new people and enjoying the thrill of wondering what special thing might happen at the game. Although I can't yet tolerate the loud noise of sporting competitions, I still put a high value on getting out and going places to create new experiences.

Our various trips have afforded us new and interesting experiences such as the stimulating flow of water in hot springs pools and the bright orange-yellow aspen leaves in the fall in Colorado, which really pop against the contrasting dark green of the pines. We've met people from far-away places, like the couple from Denmark who shared with us a fantastic view of Bear Lake with a mountain in the background. That photo is so special to me that I had it blown up and printed on canvas. It now hangs in our dining room as a 20-by-30-inch reminder of our fantastic trip. These are special experiences, and I'm so thankful we can remember them through the power of photography.

Experiences can be meaningful only because they create great memories. I remember when Carolyn lost a crown while we were on an extended walk through Anchorage, Alaska, with less than a day before leaving for a cruise; scrambling to solve that problem was both challenging and extremely satisfying once we made it through this obstacle. In Venice we walked a secluded beach hand in hand on a dark night, enjoying the view even though we wondered whether or not we were safe there. And I remember delighting in the taste of a chocolate croissant at the top of the Eiffel Tower as we stood and gazed out at the massive city of Paris. Fond memories add so much to our lives.

Learning and Growth

With my intense belief that I should work hard to be a good steward of my life, I want to develop myself to my maximum potential so I can contribute more to others. I believe this is an excellent way to honor my Creator. Just as I love to see my kids grow and maximize their abilities, I believe our heavenly Father is honored when we do all we can to use well what we have been given. In contrast, I think living a lazy life dishonors God. He has given us so much ability, and when we're idle we're not using our capabilities for good.

I have a lot of fun experiencing personal growth, especially since retiring from my corporate job. Most of my time and effort there were focused on daily survival and meeting the growth targets established by my managers. They dictated broad developmental goals that were often impossible to measure, like becoming more comfortable with ambiguity, coming across more knowledgably regarding system processes, and enhancing my executive presence. Because these goals were so intangible, my heart wasn't in it. In contrast to goals I set for myself, I felt little commitment to achieving developmental goals that were mandated by someone with a different agenda.

Since retiring I've grown tremendously in leadership, professional coaching, owning a business, networking, marketing, sales, writing and publishing, public speaking, teaching, and ninja skills. I've learned the importance of helping others with their development by providing guidelines and empowering employees to be creative in providing solutions and achieving goals.

As a professional coach I've learned the importance of drawing tailored solutions from within my client by asking open-ended questions, listening well, and being curious about their responses. As a business owner I've learned about meeting people's needs by helping them decide whether or not a service is a good investment for them. I've learned that the goal of networking is first to learn about people; if you speak to your services only when they show interest, they're more likely to remember you and share your name when they come across someone in need of what you offer.

These are subtle yet powerful differences in perspective that can make a world of difference in business. I'm very thankful that I'm a more effective business owner and coach than I was before teaching myself these skills. I love to be learning and growing in the pursuits that interest me, and will continue to create opportunities to do so.

Each day I identify and document what I learned in my journal so I can modify my perspective and/or apply it to my life going forward. I think it's really fun to keep learning about what aligns with your heart, and I believe it also honors God.

Contribution

I believe it's important to give back and help others who are on this life journey with us, including those who will come after us. The more we learn and grow, the more we can give in significant ways. Once we know how to enjoy life, we can share that with others. If we don't acquire experience, knowledge, wisdom, relationships, resources, and time, we can't give them to others. On an airplane they tell you to put your oxygen mask on first, then help children and others put theirs on; we need to be healthy and resourceful in order to contribute significantly. We can, of course, contribute while we're developing ourselves, but the more we grow the more we can give. It has been said that you can't give what you don't have.

It's important to me to contribute to my family by supporting them and spending time with them. I absolutely love helping my grandkids discover, grow, and learn new things. While on a walk through a park, I taught my granddaughter Hannah to use my binoculars. She had her own toy binoculars, but using mine took her to a whole new level.

I contribute by encouraging others at our local ninja gym and helping first-timers and others by providing information and tips about the ninja obstacles. I help family and friends, and contribute to others through social media and by coaching and mentoring. Carolyn and I give financially to organizations close to our hearts.

I give through the experiences and content in the books I've published. I'm so encouraged each time I hear from a reader about how helpful one of my books has been for them, inspiring them to be more intentional and take better care of themselves. I like to think that these contributions will continue long after I'm gone as family members and others read my books for years to come.

Prior to the coronavirus pandemic in 2020 and 2021, I contributed on a weekly basis at the Homework Help Center at the Worthington Park Library in Columbus. It was rewarding when a grade school kid discovered a new way to understand how to solve a problem, found the pattern in a math problem for the first time, or learned the definition of a new word they hadn't previously even been able to pronounce. Based on my interactions with some of their parents, I was providing a service that many foreign-born parents couldn't provide for their children. This work was extremely rewarding; I was helping others who truly needed help.

I help a bit around the house, though Carolyn carries most of the load at home. Thanks again, Dear!

I believe we're all called to serve others in some way. I'm sure you contribute to others in numerous ways, and that's worth celebrating.

All Five!

I strive to spend my time on as many of these top priorities as possible. It's a home run when an activity incorporates all five at the same time. It's been helpful to have this list to decide how to invest my time.

Each time I work on this manuscript I move a little farther along the path of spiritual wonderment. My beliefs are not identical to what I believed when I wrote the first draft. I'm being molded through each pass in the editing process. I'm even less confident about some of my beliefs, and still questioning others, but I'm thankful I'm farther down the path than I was three years ago.

Chapter 22

My Spiritual Routines

We live with a lot of routines, doing the same things over and over, often not even thinking about them. Sometimes we must be more intentional for a period in order to establish a new routine. Routines can be good or bad. My goal is to increase the good ones and eliminate the bad ones, or at least minimize them. I find my spiritual routines to be particularly beneficial.

A Worship Song in the Morning

I start most of my days by listening to a worship song or two, meditating or sometimes singing along. Today I listened to "Lord, I'm Amazed by You" by Phillips, Craig, and Dean. I closed my eyes and felt the soothing, warm sunshine. It provides a small taste of the power God packed into our star, the sun. I could have sat there a lot longer. Sometimes I listen to a third or fourth song.

This routine is a fairly new one. I've listened to worship music on occasion in the past, but not on a daily basis, at the top of the morning, with a heart of worship. This feels whole to my soul, totally focused on our Creator.

Some Scripture

I still read and meditate on some Scripture some days before starting on my to-do-list. This is the best time of my day. I get quiet and focus solely on God and who he is, by myself, not seeking to get anything from him. The more I read Scripture the more questions come to mind. Even so, I believe that regular exposure to Scripture is good and healthy and I plan to continue to read Scripture.

I've discovered that some Christians don't read Scripture regularly and hear it only in church or in a Bible study group. This is perplexing to me because I've found so much value in reading Scripture. It has been beneficial to me throughout my life and has allowed me to better know God and his heart. Reading Scripture also benefits my family members and many others I know.

Giving Thanks at Meals

As I've done since I was a child, I continue to give thanks to God at mealtimes. I approach God with a heart of thanks for the food and other necessities he provides. I don't normally ask him to do anything at mealtimes, and as you know I now don't do that at any other time either.

Moon Time

I love to sit outside at night and stare at the moon. I could do it for hours, as I've mentioned, especially when there's a full or nearly full moon. Some nights we'll be heading to bed and I'll quickly step outside and see what I can see. On clear nights when the moon is up my heart races and I have to decide whether to go to bed or head outside for a little while. Do I grab my binoculars, my tripod, and my cell phone holder for taking photos, or do I grab my camera? Or do I take my telescope, high-tech tripod, lenses, and filter case out and enjoy the views? It's easy for two hours to fly by while I'm playing with these toys, so sometimes I just look for a while and go to bed as I should. These are special times of amazement and awe at this really large object floating in space!

Earth's Timeline

I occasionally pull out my *Adams Synchronological Chart or Map of Universal History* that I mentioned earlier. It's not Scripture, or inspired by God, but it's a good summary of the timeline reflected in Scripture. I love studying it, as it helps put my life on earth in context relative to both space and time. My 64 years barely accounts for 1 percent of the 6,000-plus years mankind has been on the earth. That is not very long. Studying the chart is a new routine I enjoy regularly.

Spiritual Conversations

I enjoy meeting with others one-on-one to talk about our spiritual journeys. I try to remain open so I can gain insights that might be beneficial in my pursuit of clarity about my spiritual life. I speak as much about my recent journey as I feel comfortable sharing. If the other person is strongly black-and-white in their beliefs, I consider how open they will be to hearing about my experience before I reveal everything. It's kind of like fishing — if there's a little tug on the line I share a little more. I don't want to yank the line and totally lose them. I feel like my situation is peculiar.

I'm not trying to convince anyone of anything, but I do want to discuss my journey, my discoveries, and where they've taken me with others I can learn from. I want to know how my path is similar or different from theirs. If I were convinced that I know everything about God, I might try to be more persuasive, but avoiding that allows conversation to lead to new insights.

As I write this we are just emerging from the stay-at-home and social-distancing directives of the COVID-19 pandemic, so it's been disappointing and discouraging not to be able to talk in person with others. When I don't have opportunities to converse with others, I make less progress on my journey. This is part of the reason I started writing *Turning Gray* – as a way to share my experience with those I cannot meet with personally.

I've had some good conversations about turning gray with Carolyn, my mom, and my long-time friend Bob Valtman. I've also shared elements of my journey with non-Christian friends. As I've approached spiritual conversations over the past few years not from a black-and-white, "How can I get you to believe my way?" orientation, but from a grayer orientation, the benefits of sharing my journey have inspired me to seek out people to talk to about it on a more regular basis.

The God Cuddle Time Concept

Nearly 30 years ago I went through what I called a "God-initiated sound fast." Most people think of fasting as not eating food or certain foods for a period. I felt God had called me to a time of silence, so I called it a "sound fast." I was going to be quiet and increase my focus on God. I avoided canned sounds like TV, radio, movies, and music. Podcasts, which I sometimes listen to now, weren't even on my radar then.

I didn't feel like I was given an end date, but I felt called to start and that sometime later I would be released to again listen to sounds. My fast lasted several weeks. I was quiet when I was driving, exercising, in the evenings, and at all the times when I would typically be filling my mind with external content – songs, news, information, opinions, entertainment, stories – and I even tried to quiet my internally generated dialog.

It was really difficult. The silence was deafening. It was especially difficult to control my inner voice, and it was hard to remain open to

God while trying to be quiet. I had to fight off thoughts about my to-do list. The goal was to be available to God – to not be in to-do mode. To help chase the thoughts from my mind, sometimes I would jot a reminder note and put it by my side. But mostly I just had to fight through the mental battles to be quiet. It was a radical change, and much more challenging than any food fast I had ever tried.

Others were in my heart and on my mind during that time. I thought about family, friends, coworkers, and church group members, and their situations and status. I asked God to be with them, to provide something for them, to give them wisdom, or to encourage them. As you now know, I'm no longer asking God to take actions like this, but I did at the time. At times it was painful and extremely draining. I didn't know I could care about, or you might call it love, others so much, but I did. Things I knew were going on in their lives fell heavily to my heart. Sometimes I called them to share that they were in my thoughts, that I had prayed for them, and that I felt the need to check in.

Near the end of that fast I felt I had a deeper heart of love for others – closer to the heart that Jesus and God want us to have. This experience was the predecessor of what I now practice as "God Cuddle Time."

God Cuddle Time is a time I set aside just to be with God, alone, not rushed, not looking to get anything from him. It's his time. I'm 100 percent focused on him, as you would be with your child when they want to cuddle close to you on your favorite couch – not asking for something or talking, but conveying, "I want to spend time with you, in your presence, with your arms around me, sitting in peace and comfort." I believe our heavenly Father loves dedicated cuddle time with his Creation as much as I desire and enjoy focused cuddle time with Carolyn or our kids or grandkids.

I've shared this concept with family and friends over the years. At an early morning Bible study and prayer group that I helped lead, I explained God Cuddle Time and challenged them to try it. I started with a survey, asking how many had recently or ever dedicated as much as two or three minutes of quiet, seek-nothing-but-God time. No one raised their hand. Living busy lives, some said that they had squeezed in a little Bible reading, a prayer for someone, and maybe a worship song here and there on the drive to work, but no one had dedicated quiet time specifically with God.

Then I explained the concept and challenged them to spend three to five minutes in God Cuddle Time during the coming week. Several of them said they would give it a try.

At our next meeting I asked how it went. Most had not taken the time to try it. One person said she had tried, but she came away with nothing – she hadn't heard anything from God. I chuckled on the inside as I explained that the goal wasn't to get anything or receive anything, it was only to give God her time and attention, with nothing expected in return.

God Cuddle Time has often resulted in my coming away with a much greater perspective and an even stronger sense of awe than I had before. That's not my goal, but it's often the result. I prioritize God Cuddle Time when it feels appropriate – not as a prescribed routine. I'm sure he would love even more of it, and these days I sit in awe before him on a more regular basis. It feels right and good, and I encourage you to invest some time with your Creator in this way.

Being with God in Nature

I discussed my practice of being with God in nature above. I don't need to be with others or in a building with a certain ambiance. I only want time in his awe-inspiring Creation. Give it a try and you might be blown away by the same awe that I experience.

These are my current spiritual routines. They make a significant difference in my life. I know I'm more in love with and in awe of my Creator than ever. I love being in his creation. And I have better context for my life than ever.

Conclusion

I'm certainly a different person since my concussion, and yet I'm still the same.

Have you changed or shifted as a result of reading *Turning Gray*? If so, is that good or bad? Have you increased your pursuit of knowing God? Have you grown deeper in your relationship, knowledge, and appreciation of him?

As I shared at the beginning of the book, I'm still on my access road. I'm enjoying my life journey and I feel that I have a broader perspective now that I'm off the speedy highway and away from the bright streetlights. I continue to seek truth, knowledge, and wisdom. I've gained some clarity yet I've also raised many questions for myself, most of which I'm content to live with for the rest of my life. But I know that at times they will still concern and disturb me as I try to understand truth more fully and how best to live within it, honoring God.

I'm convinced more than ever that none of us fully understands God. I'm not sure anyone is even mostly right, including me. We simply aren't capable of knowing much of the big picture and the characteristics of God. I hope that my intense focus and effort to know God better has moved me a little closer to knowing him more deeply than I did a week, a month, a year, or 50 years ago.

I could live day to day, letting that approach dictate my time and my days. I could believe there is no God or Creator, and that we're here by chance. I could believe in one God as described by Jesus, Muhammad, and other religious leaders. I could believe there are many gods to follow or serve. Through this experience I choose to continue to follow God as he has been revealed in the Bible by Moses, Matthew, Mark, Luke, John, Paul, and others. I still believe this is our closest glimpse of the truth. Now I believe a lot more cautiously, with less confidence in my understanding of truth, yet with a stronger conviction about the fullness of God's Creation.

I hope reading about my journey has been thought-provoking and stimulating and has encouraged you to seriously seek God and truth. It's not a destination, it's a spiritual quest. I apologize that I cannot describe having landed, or where it is I hope you will journey to. I've been on this journey my entire life, and always will be. It has intensified over the past few years, and it may remain that way. The more I want to know and understand, the more questions I have. It's a long journey! I hope I've grown and I hope you are encouraged to do the same. My heart intent has been to learn and for you to be encouraged to move closer to God as you've read *Turning Gray*.

How Am I the Same?

In many ways I'm the same as I was prior to my concussion and this recent journey:

- I still believe in God and am in awe of him. I still worship him.
- I'm committed to Carolyn and my family.
- I still read the Bible regularly.
- I still believe in most of Jesus's teachings.
- I still look to Jesus to forgive my selfishness – my sin – so I can be right with God.
- I still expect to go to heaven when I die.

How Am I Different?

I've also changed in many ways. Here are some:

- I have less confidence in the message of the Bible.
- I have more unanswered questions than ever.
- My faith doesn't feel as blind as it was in the past.
- My prayers are prayers of worship and thanks. I no longer ask God for something. He knows all. He knows best.
- I'm not attending a church. I'm not aware of a church that, in my current understanding, focuses primarily on worshiping God rather than putting a significant focus on us, mankind, and surviving in this world. I would love to find a place where I can gather in unity with other worshipers of God to admire God together, both singing and learning about God through teaching.
- I'm not attending Christian gatherings. I recently joined a Christian men's group, and only went to three sessions before I needed to step away. I couldn't relate to the conversations. My new orientation makes conversations challenging.
- My confidence in Jesus as the Son of God – fully a man and fully God – is less. There are things I don't get regarding his beginning and end, his time on earth, and some of his teachings, especially in relation to asking things of God the Father. I continue to seek more understanding.

I fear being rejected by some Christians because of my new outlook on church and worship. I fear they will believe it's inappropriate to ask the questions I've been asking and to come up with the answers I've decided on. But I hope to still be able to share things we have in common outside of our spiritual beliefs. I feel many of my past beliefs have been too simple, with little if any thought behind them. I can no longer think that way.

Publishing *Turning Gray* is a bold step. It has forced me to push way beyond my fears. I'm on a journey, and I don't think God is concerned about that. I think he appreciates my being willing to move to a whole new level of honesty with him. He has been with me the whole way.

Perhaps you have discovered that you aren't alone in having spiritual questions. I hope reading about my journey encourages you to clarify your beliefs and has drawn you into a stronger desire to know our Creator.

A Life Purpose

I believe each of us has at least one primary purpose in our life that directs how we should invest our time. It might be to:

- Worship the Creator.
- Enjoy his magnificent Creation.
- Make it through each day, surviving and providing for ourselves and our families.
- Seek God's blessing, comfort, and prosperity for ourselves, our families, and our friends.
- Acquire as much land and property as we can, like Abraham and the Hebrews.
- Be an excellent steward of what we have been given.
- Create a powerful legacy.
- Evangelize and preach what we believe to others, bringing them along to our view and understanding.
- Provide for and serve others.
- Be a good steward of Creation.

The purposes that are strongest in my heart are to worship God, be an excellent steward of what he has provided, and enjoy his Creation. What is your calling? If you don't know, how you spend your time might reveal the calling you are following.

Does It Matter?

Does your belief about the Creator and Creation matter? Do we need to know where we came from and why? I believe most of our thoughts and actions stem from these big-picture beliefs. We act in accordance with our thoughts about Creation. If you believe in God, what do you believe about his interaction with people? Is he continually changing people or is he only observing? Does he hold everything together, sustaining his Creation? After death, is there an afterlife? And if so, what is it or what are the options?

When we take the time to think, we can have much deeper, well-thought-out beliefs, which lead to more confidence and a broader perspective. Deeper beliefs can help us be less dominated by the urgency that is in front of us in each moment. I think our beliefs definitely matter!

I Will Remain in Awe!

I will remain in awe, spending time being still and quiet; practicing God Cuddle Time; staring at the moon, the planets, and the stars at night; reviewing earth's timeline; worshiping with my mind, heart, voice, and sometimes my guitar; focusing on God and what he has created. You could say I'm in a "God-awe-full" place, in the true sense of these words. I am full of awe of God.

I will continue to share my heart and my journey, and I hope some will be encouraged to pursue God in a deeper way as well. By being willing to look beyond black-and-white beliefs, to appreciate the gray, and to be honest enough to ask God sincere questions to get to know him better, I have found a greater sense of awe and appreciation for our Creator. You can do this too. I believe he can handle it.

Thank you for joining me on this remarkable and sometimes confusing journey. I continue along the service road of my journey, seeking clarity and fullness of heart. Even in my uncertainty, I appreciate being on my path. I'm always open to learning and growing to see where the journey takes me. I'm a "Joe Smith," not a biblical scholar, just trying to better understand what I believe. I welcome your feedback. What am I missing? What am I overthinking? I'm available for healthy conversation that might help you along your journey as well.

I hope there will be a sequel to *Turning Gray* in which I will be able to provide answers to some my questions, gained from my continual pursuit of the truth about God and our universe!

Learn More

Contact Information

Chris Warnky, author, ninja competitor, executive and life coach, motivational speaker, trainer, and owner of Well Done Life LLC

   Cell phone: 614.787.8591 (call or text)
   Email: chriswarnky@gmail.com
   Facebook: welldonelife
   Website: welldone-life.com
   Blog: http://cwarnky.wordpress.com

Be Coached by Chris

Chris provides both executive and life coaching.

Be Mentored by Chris Using the 12 Traits of a Ninja

Chris offers "Twelve Trait Mentoring" (from his book *The Heart of a Ninja*), which can be ideal for young people who love *American Ninja Warrior* and could benefit from a strong male presence in their lives.

Thirteen percent of the profits from sales of Chris's books are donated to charitable organizations.

Acknowledgments

I'm thankful to our awesome Creator/God for allowing me to live 64 years and for providing me with many wonderful relationships and experiences. I'm also thankful to have peace with him.

Thanks to my wife, Carolyn, for your love, and especially for your support while I've been writing, editing, and publishing this and other books – especially *Turning Gray,* which has been so deep and personal for both of us. I can't imagine going through anything without you. I love you!

Thanks to those who have shared that they are intrigued by this topic and my journey. And to those who have asked me to share what I learn because they've had some of the same thoughts.

There are countless others I'm thankful to because of their contributions to my life, and for their help with the writing, editing, and feedback for *Turning Gray*. Specifically I'd like to thank my mom and dad for the love and support you've provided throughout my life. Thanks to Tim and Bonnie and Michelle and Joel for continually supporting me during my interesting life journey.

Thanks also to Shanon Paglieri for your continual support and encouragement, especially with this extremely transparent, deep, and personally challenging manuscript.

Thanks to Gwen Hoffnagle, my professional editor for my first eight books. You continue to take my original manuscripts to new and much higher levels. I enjoy working with you and appreciate the value you provide. Thank you so much!

About the Author

Chris Warnky is 64 years young and has been married to Carolyn for over 42 years. He has two adult children, both living in Ohio.

Chris is a ninja warrior, following in the footsteps of his daughter, Michelle Warnky Buurma. He competed in the 2017 *American Ninja Warrior Cleveland City Qualifier*, and he's a Movement Lab Ohio (MLAB OH) staff member.

Chris has been a Bible-reading Christian for over 50 years. His relationship with God is the basis for his life.

He is a multi-book author, a professional executive and life coach, and a thought-provoking speaker through his business, Well Done Life.

He is a certified coach, speaker, and trainer with the John Maxwell Team. He served two years on the organization's President's Advisory Council. He served two terms as the International Coach Federation Columbus Charter Chapter president.

Chris has over three decades of corporate leadership experience, including 23 years as a vice president at Bank One/JP Morgan Chase contributing as a compensation manager, project manager, and program manager.

Made in the USA
Las Vegas, NV
09 September 2021